Is human consciousness designed for self-destruction?

OR

Is it designed to continuously sustain its own pro-survival into futurity?

There are many categories within human consciousness that work to sustain pro-survival. But all of them can be affiliated with one central header: WISDOM, without which our species could not have survived anything, even itself...

Ingo Swann (1933-2013) was an American artist and exceptionally successful subject in parapsychology experiments. As a child he spontaneously had numerous paranormal experiences, mostly of the OBE type, the future study of which became a major passion as he matured. In 1970, he began acting as a parapsychology test subject in tightly controlled laboratory settings with numerous scientific researchers. Because of the success of most of these thousands of test trials, major media worldwide often referred, to him as "the scientific psychic." His subsequent research on behalf of American intelligence interests, including that of the CIA, won him top PSI-spy status.

His involvement in government research projects required the discovery of innovative approaches toward the actual realizing of subtle human energies. He viewed PSI powers as only parts of the larger spectrum of human sensing systems and was internationally known as an advocate and researcher of the exceptional powers of the human mind.

To learn more about Ingo, his work, art and other books, please visit: **www.ingoswann.com.**

THE WISDOM CATEGORY

SHEDDING LIGHT ON A LOST
LIGHT

A BIOMIND SUPERPOWERS BOOK
PUBLISHED BY

Swann-Ryder Productions, LLC
www.ingoswann.com

For more information address: www.ingoswann.com.

Previously published in trade paperback by Ingo Swann Books and Crossroad Press and digitally by Crossroad Press.

First edition BioMind Superpowers Books.

Cover art: *Pyramid* by Ingo Swann © Swann-Ryder Productions, LLC.

Triangle icon from www.flaticon.com.

ISBN-13: 978-1-949214-77-2

THE WISDOM CATEGORY

CATEGORY

INGO SWANN

WHAT IS THE ACTUAL NATURE AND PURPOSE OF WISDOM?

UNLESS one knows what something can be used for, it has no meaning. What has no meaning is often not perceived at all.

There are many traditions implying that wisdom can exist. There are some generalizing dictionary definitions for it. But WHEN these definitions are in hand, one can look around and not actually perceive wisdom as existing – because what it can be used for has not been recognized as such.

Thus, wisdom remains theoretical but not evidential. Even those (few) philosophers who (briefly) consider wisdom tend to miss (or avoid) the meaningful link between wisdom and what it can evidentially be used for.

In his wonderful book published in 1964 entitled POWER TRANSFORMED, the renowned social scientist Robert M. MacIver (1882-1970) mentioned that: "In human affairs there is often a fatal disproportion between the ends men seek and the consequences of their seeking."

FATAL refers to entanglements or miscalculations "bringing ruin" or "causing death" relevant to smaller- or bigger-picture situations – which rose to their all-time high during the twentieth century, during which even theoretical discussions of wisdom fell to their all-time low. However, it doesn't take too much imagination to figure out that "fatal disproportion" comes about because of lack of a lost light that needs new illumination focused on it.

Dedication

Silliness, utter lack of principle, villainy, harshness, turbulence, and recklessness are historically infamous for the absence of wisdom.

The discussions in this book are dedicated to those who might seek to open the many doors of wisdom that are innate in human consciousness.

Contents

Author's Note

A SOMEWHAT EXTENSIVE "wisdom literature" does exist, the larger part of which deals with wisdom of the ancients, wisdom aphorisms and metaphors, and various occult and metaphysical constructs about it. There are very many treasures to be found throughout this larger part.

The same can be said about the smaller part of the literature, as found in sources such as biographies, autobiographies, and teaching texts which, in the cultural West, sporadically appeared between the Renaissance epoch and the end of the nineteenth century.

With the exception of certain valuable ancient Eastern sources, wisdom and wisdom-making have not been examined from within the contexts of human consciousness as a whole.

This was certainly the case during the modern period in which wisdom had almost no place in science, psychology, sociology, philosophy, or in studies of intelligence, mind, and brain.

Yet, if and when wisdom comes forth, or emerges, it does so from resources somewhere and somehow residing in the manifold depths of human consciousness.

The discussions in this book attempt to spot some of these resources, at least at a preliminary level, and to connect them together as adjuncts or patterns supportive of wisdom-making. Some of the topics introduced might at first seem far removed from that of wisdom and hard to connect to its substance.

There are always problems with nomenclature and words that have multiple meanings. To help ease such problems, unless otherwise indicated, this author has tenaciously depended on established definitions of English words, the sum of which, rather surprisingly, reveals that the English language already possesses an existing wisdom vocabulary, although it is rarely used as such.

Preface

DURING MY CHILDHOOD years, of wisdom was considered important and the phrase "Let wisdom guide all our undertakings" was often heard from pulpit, in prayers, and in school and civic meetings.

I don't remember how wisdom was actually defined back then. But I do remember that its existence was thought to be as real as the sun and moon, although via chatter and gossip it was said to be beyond the reach of types referred to as simpletons, the foolhardy, the inexperienced, the greedy, and those who were "too full of themselves to know better."

"My childhood," as I tabulate it, probably ended somewhere during the dismal course of World War II. That war also ended the Age of Progress that had gotten underway about thirty or so years earlier, during which it was broadly predicted that the knowledge-wisdom emerging from the developing sciences would create a Utopia by the year 2000.

The end of World War II was quickly followed by a new Age - the Atomic and Nuclear Age - chiefly characterized by the advent of weapons of mass destruction.

Since these had been born out of the developing sciences, it suggested, to some, the notion that the developing sciences didn't have a very good grip on wisdom, which notion was socially embarrassing more or less across the boards. There is a general tendency to sweep whatever is embarrassing under this or that carpet. Thus, during the 1950s, wisdom (rather, the lack of it) was made to "disappear" as a meaningful form of study and development.

I remember it being said that whatever wisdom might consist of, it constituted one of the highest apexes that human consciousness might aspire to. This somehow got lodged in my little gray cells and must account for my continuing interest in the topic ever since. Now that I am in the latter part of my own life cycle, I have decided to record what I have become aware of about wisdom and wisdom-making.

In the early 1960s, I began to examine how wisdom was, in general, treated worldwide and in various cultures and societies.

Among other sources, this effort required reading various dictionaries and encyclopedias, and eventually a strange situation became visible.

Because of its obvious importance (theoretically speaking, anyway) one might assume that there is a big wisdom literature in existence. But such is not really the case – if compared, for example, to the plethora of books dealing with gardening, cooking, interior decorating, war, sex, astronomy, pesticides, crime, how to get what you want, how to influence people, and so forth.

There are NO educational curricula (no Wisdom 101s) anywhere that might nurture wisdom, and there is no concise history of it. What one finds instead is that when wisdom is mentioned (as some philosophers do), it is only in passing and usually via some kind of proverb or aphorism that hints of it but says not much more.

Although some encyclopedias do not bother with a mention of wisdom, the otherwise usually excellent Encyclopedia of Philosophy (1967) does have an entry for it. However, it mostly focuses (if briefly and weakly) on the wisdom of the ancient Greek philosophers, and even more weakly refers to some few modern philosophers. The short bibliography accompanying the entry does not mention any books about it. Instead, it refers to:

Proverbs and Their Lessons (1858) by R.C. Trench;
How We Think (1910) by John Dewey;
Rational Living (1912) by H.C. King;
The Rational Good (1921) by L. T. Hobhouse;
The Proverb (1931), by Arch Taylor;
The Uses of Reason (1943) by A.E. Murphy;
Reasonable Living (1948) by T.E. Jessop;
Reason and Goodness (1962) by Brand Blanshard;
The Methods of Ethics (1962) by Henry Sidgwick.

So, although books about reason, rationality, ethics, and goodness are pointed up in the Encyclopedia, no books about wisdom itself are referred to.

The foregoing constitutes a rough, if incomplete, sketch of the general understanding about and status of wisdom during, say, the last two hundred years during which it has seldom prevailed anywhere. It can thus be assumed that wisdom, if it does come into existence, has factors that have seldom, if ever, been brought to light.

History, science and philosophy all make
us aware of the great collective achievements
of mankind.

It would be well if every civilized
human being had a sense of these
achievements and a realization of the possibility
of greater things to come, with the indifference
which must result as regards the petty squabbles
upon which the passions of individuals and nations
are wastefully squandered.

Bertrand Russell (1872-1970)

PART ONE

WISDOM AS A SERIES OF ENIGMAS

Chapter One

CAN YOU READ THE SIGNS?

1

IT IS TRADITIONALLY accepted that the human species possesses capacities for producing, evolving, or making wisdom. Nevertheless, history shows that it is produced only sporadically, and even then, what COULD have served as wisdom is better seen in retrospect, after the bam has burned down, so to speak. In other words, humans have capacities to produce wisdom, and then not utilize it.

This is an enigma – something puzzling, hard to understand or explain. So, examples are needed, some of which are found in a book entitled THE GREATEST DISASTERS OF THE 20™ CENTURY, by Frances Kennett, published in 1975.

In the book's Introduction, the author points up that disasters are the result of natural phenomena that are unaffected by the actions of mere human beings. Modern technology is capable of predicting hurricanes, tornadoes, and even earthquakes. But the warnings are ignored to a notorious degree even when becoming self-evident. The real disaster, in terms of human life, almost always comes from this uniquely human failure to heed the signs.

2

The volcano called Mont Pelee near the town of St. Pierre on the tropical island of Martinique in the Caribbean began erupting in earnest in late April, 1902. Known to be an active volcano, the new eruptions were nevertheless thought of as a curiosity and as a possible tourist attraction.

Even as St. Pierre and its local surroundings began to be covered with sulfuric white ash, a scientific commission was sent up to investigate. The commission's finding was that there was nothing to fear.

The local main newspaper published this finding, and in several editorials thereafter, even mocked those citizens who were beginning to express fears. Soon, the ash and gases increased. Dead birds began falling out of the vaporous sky, and horses dropped dead asphyxiated by the ash and sulfuric fumes.

This alone was reason enough, and some 300 a day began leaving. But these were replaced by an influx of people coming in from neighboring villages.

On May 8, Pelee's activities grew ultra-ominous, and the volcano did its main thing at 8.05 in the morning. A flow of flame and glistening superheated steam (at about 1500 degrees Fahrenheit) speeded down the volcanic slopes engulfing and, in minutes, destroyed St. Pierre and the vessels in its harbor. The ultimate death toll was set at 30,000.

The "signs" had been entirely visible for several days, unread by 30,000, including St. Pierre's officials apparently seeking to preserve the town's economy in the face of the quite foreseeable ominous consequences.

This is not the only example of massively lapsed common sense wisdom. On April 14, 1912, the famous "unsinkable" ship TITANIC collided with an iceberg in the North Atlantic, the collision being blamed as the cause of the sinking. But the sinking actually occurred because one human after another failed to heed the signs of danger presented by an ominous pack of icebergs in the ship's path. As a consequence, 1,503 passengers and crew perished.

Such deadly consequences come about with respect to manmade disasters. World Wars I and II were preceded by multitudes of signs that were indeed recognized by some but were explained away or ignored by very many more – and clearly because high-placed men were more interested in the ends they sought, with almost no concern for the consequences of their seeking, which consequences entailed multiple millions of dead and wasted.

3

In both natural and manmade disasters, attention goes to the magnitudes and details of the disasters, while the consequences are merely attributed to stupidity.

The point being made here refers not just to the grizzly details of the disasters and the stupidity involved, but to one of the more subtle enigmas that surrounds wisdom. This enigma is so enigmatic that it almost defies any linguistic expression of it.

First, there is an old saying that "the future always foreshadows itself" via signs or signals of what is to come.

Second, it is an accepted full part of wisdom to notice and take account of such signs.

Third, human intelligence is considered one of the superlative attributes of our species, intelligence sufficient enough to recognize (theoretically anyway) disasters in the making.

Fourth, however, there are no educational courses that might be called Recognition of Signs 101.

4

One of the established definitions of SIGN is given as "something that serves to indicate the presence or existence of something" – such as present or forthcoming danger. Synonyms are given as symptom, mark, token, presage, portent, warning, and premonition – extended by metaphors such as bird of ill omen, gathering clouds, put on one's guard, heed at one's peril, signs of the times ahead, and so forth.

These definitions are workable enough to establish an educational course of Signs 101 and sufficient enough to at least intellectually establish the basic reality of signs and signals.

Such might help in recognizing the reality meaning of sulfuric ash piling up and icebergs all around and just ahead – realities confirmed to have been almost totally absent when Mont Pelee did its awesome thing, and when the "unsinkable" TITANIC sank.

Somewhere in the above discussion is one or more of the subtle enigmas that surround wisdom which are partly described by the following formula: No Signs 101, no intellectual reality awareness about them causing the banishment of wisdom (and common sense), resulting in the signs of the times just ahead to do their things.

This formula indicates the existence of something more than mere stupidity and is more suggestive of insufficient education about the reality of signs. If this is the case, then there is also insufficient education with respect to awareness, intelligence, wisdom, and especially that enigmatic thing they emerge out of – human consciousness itself.

5

In a certain and uncomplicated sense, wisdom can be thought of as doing the right thing at the right time. When this works out, there is little more to say.

However, the nomenclature background for our English term WISDOM shows that it is derived from Old English WIS and WISSIAN which meant "to make known, to give information of, to indicate, especially to show or point out the way."

In contrast, our modern definitions of WISDOM are given as: "accumulated philosophic or scientific learning: knowledge: ability to discern inner qualities and relationships: insight; good sense and judgment; a wise attitude or course of action; and [lastly] the teachings of the ancient wise men."

6

A subtle distinction between the modern definitions and the Old English one is that the modern ones might or might NOT result in wisdom (as seems to have been the case with accumulated philosophic or scientific learning, the sum of which proved insufficient with respect to pointing out the way whereby the excessive conflicts, horrors, holocausts, and body counts of the twentieth century might have been avoided).

So, gasping the functional nature of wisdom depends not only on what we think wisdom needs to consist of, but also on what it is to be used for. If wisdom cannot be used to point out the way (in the constructive positive sense), then what it otherwise consists doesn't matter too much.

An implication of all of this is that there yet remain some

awesome unknowns about additional factors that might contribute to functional wisdom-making.

Chapter Two

AWESOME ENIGMAS

7

A UNIVERSAL characteristic of our species has to do with the tendency of peoples to live within the contexts of what they know, or think they do. This tendency can easily be observed and confirmed at the individual and collective levels.

This is all well and good enough – since it means that most can get along through their lives within the contexts of what they know and are usually content enough to do so – until they encounter something that has been unknown to them.

There is an old adage that is often applied to this kind of thing: the more one knows, the more it is increasingly realized what is unknown – and, in certain cases, what is finally perceived as unknown can take on awesome proportions.

One of the cognitive fallouts of the foregoing is that if something is unknown it doesn't exist as having reality unless, or until, it is PERCEIVED as being unknown.

This implies that people can easily live within what is known to them while living concurrently within what is unknown, without realizing it. But is seems that the larger or more awesome an unknown is, the less likely it will be perceived as such, if at all.

8

There are many awesome unknowns that can suddenly pop into view, not often at the average level of living, but at the cutting edges of the really hard sciences – say, of advancing physics, astrophysics, biology, and neurology – in which theories of what IS are shifting about all of the time.

In recent times, this has especially been the case of

astrophysics which, fifty years ago, had established certainty about what the cosmos fundamentally consisted of. As was the comparable case in Classical Physics during the late eighteenth century, only the remaining details of the cosmos needed to be wrapped up.

However, the process of wrapping up details began revealing what was not known about the cosmos – with the result that most previous theories and understanding became increasingly wobbly and uncertain – especially with respect to its origins and dimensions and its evolutional and dynamic forces, all of which remain unresolved and enigmatic.

9

Meanwhile, back on Earth, there exists an awesome and very enigmatic unknown that everyone intimately lives not only with and among, but also interactively shares with others.

It is said that someone once asked a fish to describe everything in its environment, and the fish responded by describing everything but the water.

In a similar fashion, if one asks a human specimen to describe its environment, a long list of this or that will download, and the chances are very good that consciousness will not appear on the list.

Like the fish's water, consciousness is the FIRST environmental aspect a human specimen exists within. Absent water = no fish. Absent consciousness = no human specimen.

Indeed, no human consciousness = no species called Homo sapiens sapiens (i.e., Man who knows and knows that he knows).

10

Most modern dictionaries define CONSCIOUNESS in the following order:

1. Awareness, especially of something within oneself;
2. The state or fact of being conscious of an external object, state or fact;
3. The state of being characterized by sensation, emotion, volition, and thought (MIND);

4. The totality of conscious states of an individual;
5. The upper level of mental life as contrasted with unconscious processes.

On average, concepts of consciousness are based only on the second and third definitions above. This implies that being "conscious of" something is consciousness itself.

But this cannot be the case, because to become "conscious of" something requires, shall we say, a deeper background of faculties that permit becoming "conscious of" something to take place.

The first definition above begins with the word "awareness," that term usually being thought of as "awareness of" something. But in the same way, "awareness of" something can only be possible against a deeper background of faculties that permit it to take place.

11

One of the difficulties here is that the -NESS part of the word "consciousness" does not refer to things one may, or may not, become aware or conscious of. Rather, it is a suffix meaning "state; condition; quality; or degree."

QUALITY is defined as: "an inherent feature, property, or capacity, or natural attribute" all of which terms apply to whatever is inborn from the get-go.

In this sense, the "backdrop" referred to above is composed of innate features, properties, capacities, or attributes that permit this or that "awareness of" and "conscious of" to take place.

In its deeper meaning, therefore, human consciousness per se is not composed ONLY of what one becomes aware or conscious of – this being an issue that will be much discussed in the text ahead. Thus, the "deeper" innateness of human consciousness constitutes one of the more awesome unknowns we are all enigmatically living with and among.

12

The third definition of CONSCIOUSNESS is given as "the

state of being [that is] characterized by sensation, emotion, volition, and thought" – i.e., MIND.

When wisdom occurs, it is commonly thought to be a product of MIND. This can be the case only in some ideal metaphysical sense, largely because our species has minds everywhere, most of which are not all that notable for producing too much wisdom.

Wisdom is therefore expected to transcend minds in some way – to transcend "sensation, emotion, volition, and thought" of minds that cannot of and in themselves produce, evoke, or evolve wisdom.

13

Thus, if the "mind" thing is deleted, hypothetically anyway, from the wisdom scenario, it can appear that we are left without any understanding of its essential nature and how it can come about.

But this is not actually the case because the term WISDOM has always denoted a special category of human activity that shares something in common with other special categories whose essential nature is not understood, but which are fully accepted as existing anyway. For example, those categories we refer to as creativity, inventiveness, innovation, intuitiveness, imaginative skill, and intelligence, all of which have transcending potentials.

While it is generally accepted that these categories can benefit from learning and experience, it is agreed that their fundamental sources or origins are as obscure and enigmatic as are those of wisdom. Like wisdom, they are judged by what they produce. Like wisdom, they are judged by what they produce. But otherwise the fundamental main-springs behind, anterior, or coming before what they produce are "hidden" and thus invisible.

Even so, the main-springs, if invisible, have traditionally been referred to via numerous metaphors that are packaged together as GENERATIVE in nature.

Descriptive terms such as egg, germ, embryo, fetus, bud, tap-root, nucleus, seed, latent organism, breeding-place, evolved-from, core, and womb have collectively been seized upon to give reference to their inherent, source-causative nature of mainsprings.

(In contrast, it is helpful to note that the opposite of generative is degenerative, which has its own metaphors – such as deterioration, debasement, decay, ebb, recession, retrogradation, decrease, degradation, retrogression, loss, havoc, contamination, corruption, and demoralization, etc.)

Each of the special categories are commonly thought to be generative in nature, especially the wisdom category, the workings of which are thought of as optimizing the best chances of survival and right action among all that is degenerative and thus counter-survival.

The wisdom category also shares something else in common with the other special categories – the idea that they and then – products are exclusively functions of some little understood indwelling intelligence whose nature is entirely enigmatic.

Chapter Three

UPDATES ON THE ENIGMATIC STRUCTURE OF INTELLIGENCE

14

SOME PROGRESS has taken place during the last fifty or so years with respect to increasing knowledge about one of the greater enigmatic unknowns - that of intelligence. If intelligence and  wisdom are closely linked, any advances that illuminate the former have implications toward comprehending the latter.

One of the definitions of INTELLIGENCE is given as: "the capacity to apprehend facts and propositions and their relations and to reason about them." This definition is also applicable to information processing of any kind, and, in part, to wisdom.

15

It is a rather strange story as to how advances in understanding more about intelligence have come about – in that the advances have been not been made in psychological study, but in the field of designing artificial intelligence.

To wit, the ever-increasing refinements of computers demanded that they be programmed so as to internally have information processing capacities, and therefore be more artificially "intelligent" as smart systems.

The whole of this, of course, is quite complicated. However, it is discussed and more or less simplified in a book entitled DESIGNING INTELLIGENCE – A FRAMEWORK FOR SMART SYSTEMS (1990), by Steven H. Kim, a professor of mechanical engineering at M.I.T.

Containing informative graphs and charts, more details about intelligence are found in this book than anywhere else, it serves as a boundary marker more or less putting an end to all that was inefficiently known about intelligence in the past.

16

In brief review and slightly paraphrased, Kim indicates that artificial intelligent systems can be designed and programmed so as to display a range of behaviors that can be viewed as the means to an objective, as would be the case with robots designed to perform certain specific tasks, or with computers that can sift thousands of data bits.

The purpose of an engineered intelligent system is specifically defined by the goals of the designer – whereas natural animate intelligent systems pursue an innate, self-internal hierarchy of goals, chief among which is the survival of the self and the species.

Additionally, the behavior of an artificially designed intelligent system is to fulfill its purpose without incurring deleterious side effects, and so the environment (or space) involved must be clearly delineated and the modes of action properly implemented with respect to patterns of interaction.

Whether artificial or natural, an intelligent system interacts with its environment through a series of processes, which can be classified as primary functions and supporting activities. The primary functions depend on supporting processes, such as intrasystem communication networks.

If the elements of the foregoing are a little hard to cognitively take on board, don't worry too much, because they will become more apparent throughout the text ahead.

17

The desire to engineer or fabricate artificially intelligent systems and machines is now about forty or so years along, and examples of them range from improved "smart" security and even "smarter" surveillance systems, finger-print ident equipment, and "smart" bombs and missiles, etc.

Somewhere during the 1980s, those up-to-date on scientific trends began predicting that computer programming, artificial intelligence design, genetic engineering, and nanotechnology would become interdependent and ultimately merge together because their activities were all interconnected. Of these four sciences, nanotechnology is now surfacing as the most significant.

NANO simply refers to a 1 billionth part of something, or, in nanotechnology, to enlarging a really tiny something a billion times via powerful microscopes and other detecting equipment, which permits easy identification of the structures and nanoparticles of molecules including their atoms.

Once nanoparticles can be identified, it becomes possible to manipulate them, first in theory and then by experimentation, the results of which help redesign the theories which then lead to better and more productive forms of experimentation.

So, nanotechnology involves the study of discovering ways and means of manipulating nanoparticles so as to achieve altered or new combinations of atoms that might result in new, artificial forms of molecules.

18

At present, like the designing of artificial intelligent systems and equipment, nanotechnology is still mostly a materials technology. However, in nanobiological technology and nanogenetic manipulation, the focus is generally drifting toward technologies aimed at building artificial self-reproducing substances and entities.

Via nanogenetic manipulation, for example, genetic structures could be altered at nanogenetic levels to start up self-reproducing entities whose characteristics would then proliferate in whatever environment could act as host for them.

Such self-reproducing entities could (in THEORY as it is said so far), even manifest themselves as self-reproducing artificial life creatures having their own life-survival purposes and goals.

Expanding on this particular situation is the novel by Michael Crichton entitled PREY (2002). This fiction is a gripping read, in which one learns much about nanotechnology and some few of its awesome and ominous implications.

A similar and now familiar example of self-replicating entities has to do with computer "viruses" or computer "worms" which are generally composed of a series of code or algorithm that self-reproduce when introduced into a computer system, sometimes creating massive destruction within them.

Certainly, one of the usually not emphasized goals of nanobiological, nanogenetic, and even nanochemical technologies is to explore feasibilities of bio/chemical self-proliferating weapons of mass destruction. The effort is said to be only theoretical so far, but it is hard to think that pursuits in this direction have not already commenced here and there.

19

It is interesting to note that like innovators of intelligent machines, who had to figure out what such machines basically required to be intelligent, it transpired that nanotechnologists had to figure out what artificial life needs in order to basically function as such.

And in this sense, it turns out that although there are certain strategic differences between them, the basics of both artificial intelligent machines, artificial intelligent life, AND naturally intelligent life have much in common.

Chapter Four

THE ENIGMA OF OPTIMIZATION OF INTELLIGENCE

20

THERE IS A KEY CONCEPT that needs to be somewhat broadened out in order to understand such basic needs.

This is the concept of OPTIMIZATION defined as: "to make as perfect, effective, efficient, and functional as possible."

In the case of designing intelligent machines, they somehow need to be programmed with factors having to do with purpose, space (environment), structure, time, process, memory, and efficient behavior. It turns out that these six factors are also components of life intelligence per se.

However, artificial self-reproducing life, if it is to be self-sustaining, also needs to:

1) learn from experience;
2) have collective memory at its fundamental levels;
3) have and exchange collective intelligence among the collective sum of its molecule elements; and
4) must be somehow able to innovate (or self-evolve) to solve problems it encounters.

(Please bear in mind the context of (3) above, which will figure significantly in the text ahead.)

21

By considering the basic needs of artificial intelligent machines and artificially engineered life forms, we learn more about what intelligence needs in order to optimize on it. And so at least some few factors of that awesome unknown called intelligence have been brought to light.

22

While all of these basic intelligence needs have been drawn from impeccable scientific sources (not from philosophical or psychological ones), there is one basic factor that has not been mentioned in the scientific sources regarding artificial intelligent machines or artificial engendered life.

It is a factor that has made an appearance in computer technology: highly sophisticated computer systems can analyze incoming data against their memory stored data, and can make relevant predictions about the incoming data, although such predictions are only as good as is the scope of the stored memory data.

We cannot of course expect that mere artificial intelligent machines can do too much with regard to predicting, although some have been programmed to issue alerts, ring bells, etc., when situations under their auspices have begun to change.

But with respect to artificial life, such would need some kind of predictive capacities in addition to, or embedded in, its other intelligence capacities.

After all, intelligent life would not be too intelligent if it could not have and respond to, by some means or another, a sense of prediction.

23

In any event, in the whole human world, which is infinitely bigger than its sciences so far, having the sense of prediction AND responding to it is not only thought to reflect high-intelligence, but is called WISDOM.

In general, then:
SOME STRUCTURAL ELEMENTS
(OF SIMPLE ARTIFICIAL INTELLIGENCE)
Purpose
Space
Structure
Time
Process
Efficiency
(OF MORE COMPLEX ARTIFICIAL INTELLIGENCE)
Purpose
Space
Structure
Time
Process
Memory
Detection-sensing systems relevant to space-environment,
process functioning, and purpose
Designed reason-logic capacities in keeping with purpose and
intrasystem networks
Designed capacities relevant
to avoiding deleterious side effects
Self-learning patterns
Efficiency

(OF ARTIFICAL LIFE INTELLIGENCE)

All of the above

PLUS

Learn from experience
Have collective memory at its fundamental levels Have and
exchange collective intelligence among the collective sum of its
molecule elements and intranetworks
Must be somehow be able to innovate (or self-evolve) to solve
problems it encounters.
(OF NATURAL, EVOLVING LIFE INTELLIGENCE)

All of the above

PLUS

Innate capacities for:
Self-internal organization
Self-ordering among randomness or disorder
Self-reproduction
Predictability functions
Self-determinism
Powers of interface complexity
Versatility
Detection systems
Deduction systems
Innate formative skills specific to intelligence
Systemic flexibility
Sensory molecular, motor, and intelligence receptors
responding to environmental stimuli
Innate strategy patterns relevant to achieving purposes, goals,
or objectives
Innate prediction systems supportive of intuition, deduction,
sensing outcomes, and foresight
Sensing systems differentiating between deleterious and non-
deleterious side-effects

(Please note that some items on the life-intelligence list can be
in a recessive condition but are nevertheless ancestor-memory
innate in all self-replicating life-intelligence units.)

(Please ALSO note that all of the foregoing lists must be thought
of as incomplete.)

Chapter Five

A FACTOR OF INTELLIGENT LIFE THAT IS CONSISTENTLY AVOIDED

24

IN HIS FAMOUS book entitled ON THE ORIGINS OF SPECIES (first published in 1859), Charles Darwin (1809-1882) wrote:

> "Every detail of structure in every living creature (making some little allowance for the direct action of physical conditions) may be viewed, either as having been of special use to some ancestral form, or as being now of special use to the descendants of this form – either directly, or indirectly through the complex laws of growth."

During the modern period, it was generally held that what may have "been of special use to some ancestral form" of our human species was, so to speak, somehow terminated or eliminated when it was no longer useful, and thus ceased to be inherited by subsequent generations.

25

Although such might be the case, this concept runs counter to the human species genome whose ongoing innate characteristics are replicated and inherited in its successive generations. Indeed, one of the definitions of INHERITANCE is given as: "the possession, condition, or trait from past generations."

The concept also runs counter to the process via which organic life builds itself, and which processes consist of some form of memory – more or less, perhaps, in the same way that computers rely on installed past and new memory bits.

26

There are two definitions of MEMORY that are pertinent to this particular discussion: (1) The power or process of reproducing or recalling what has been learned and retained, especially through associated mechanisms; and (2) Persistent modification of structure or behavior resulting from an organism's activity or experience.

Now, with respect to computers at least, memory cannot be junked and eradicated if it becomes temporarily useless. Doing so would decrease and degrade both scope and identification of memory overall so that the computations within the computer would not be able to identify what is useless.

Indeed, and all things considered, useless memory might again become useful for various reasons.

27

This can be translated over to the case of intelligent organic life. Such is accepted as replicating itself via various kinds of simple cellular memory patterns on upward to more complex forms of them. So, it is difficult to see why any kind of species self-replicating memory should cease to exist as such in subsequent generations.

Admittedly, memory no longer directly useful could become recessive memory, archaic memory, or stored as some kind of zipped file memory. But various conditions subsequent generations might encounter might unzip such files, thereby opening them up to accessible memory.

28

Species formative memory is referred to as being INNATE, three definitions being:

1. belonging to the intrinsic nature of something;
2. existing in or belonging to an individual from birth; and
3. a quality or tendency either actually present at birth or so marked and deep-seated as to seem so.

So, although one doesn't want to put words into the mouth of the venerable Charles Darwin, when he speaks of "some ancestral form," it could be inferred that it has to do with various kinds of innate memory downloading into subsequent generations, albeit if only in some recessive form.

Since Darwin's time, such memory has been variously referred to as "archaic," "non-conscious," "subconscious," and "unconscious" memory. This topic has been early opened up here, because, as will be discussed in the text ahead, it has something to do with possible sources of wisdom.

Chapter Six

TWO PRINCIPAL LAMENTS ABOUT THE LACK OF WISDOM

29

THERE IS the old saying that when history is forgotten, it repeats itself, and this is broadly lamented.

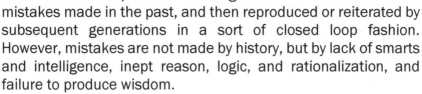

On the surface, this seems largely to refer to the repetition of forgotten mistakes made in the past, and then reproduced or reiterated by subsequent generations in a sort of closed loop fashion. However, mistakes are not made by history, but by lack of smarts and intelligence, inept reason, logic, and rationalization, and failure to produce wisdom.

So, when the same or similar mistakes repeat in subsequent historical epochs, it can be deduced that what is repeating are various lacks, ineptitudes, and failures of reason, logic, intelligence, and awareness.

One seeming reason that we do not learn too much from past historical mistakes is that history is almost solely conceptualized as the record of human activities that translated into the events that took place, while mistakes that played roles in the activities are seldom dissected in understandable terms.

An end result of this is that although there is a history of events, there is no real history of human mistakes, and unless these can frankly and intimately be dissected, described, and rendered understandable, then few in subsequent generations can learn anything about them.

30

The foregoing leads into the second general lament about the lack of wisdom, elements of which have appeared since ancient times, and which indeed figure in many parables and aphorisms of wisdom.

In general, people feel they know what they are doing, and always have.

However, few seem to acknowledge how and why people have been intrinsically wrong in the past, and, as noted by Michael Crichton in the Introduction to his novel PREY, such errors are explained away as merely bad thinking by less able minds in the past.

After all, "We" are here now, and we are confident that we know what we are doing – and equally confidently we embark on fresh errors of our own, errors equally lacking wisdom.

31

In a broader reality, people cannot really KNOW what they are doing. They can only assume that they do. Sometimes the assumptions turn out to have actual and real value. But otherwise, assumptions are better known as the principal sources of all F-ups.

Thus, although artificial intelligence might be innovated and designed along clear-cut lines that more or less flawlessly lead to optimization of its purposes and goals, human intelligence (and thus its wisdom-making potentials) remains rather cluttered with "thinking" in ways that are random, vicissitudinous, and sometimes wild enough to act as deterrents to efficient wisdom-making.

32

For tentative discussion purposes only, below are some examples of thinking and thinking patterns that might either enhance or degrade wisdom-making. Readers might undertake adding items of their own since such examples are numerous in the extreme.

It is possible that potentials of wisdom-making can be rated on a scale ranging from one to ten (1-10), zero indicating no wisdom-making at all. Ten might indicate achieved wisdom-making, and/or high optimization of it.

The mid-point on this scale might indicate the make-break point between what enhances generative wisdom and what degenerates it.

After all of the examples or items have been given a rating ranging from one to ten, the counts can simply be averaged out so that a combined overall value can be determined. Please note that this is just an exercise.

- Thinking that avoids or obviates what is unknown but could be known.
- Thinking within the contexts of correct ideas.
- Thinking within the terms of pseudo or false ideas.
- Thinking in terms of generative factors and elements.
- Thinking in terms of degenerative factors and elements.
- Lack of recognition between generative and degenerative factors.
- Recognition of generative and degenerative elements.
- Thinking patterns and systems that produce deleterious side effects.
- Lack of optimizing all levels of consciousness.
- Thinking patterns characteristic of various types of reality boxes and mentally clinging to them.
- Inability to recognize the nature of mistakes.
- Ability to recognize the nature of mistakes.
- Artificial or socially-designed limits to innate intelligence.
- Too much focus on negative human activities, potentials, and activities.
- Not enough focus on positive human activities, potentials, and activities.
- Failure to recognize the strategic differences between negative and positive human capacities.
- Fascination with destruction (of any and all kinds).
- Interest in pro-creativity.
- Incapacity in predicting reason-logic failures.
- Capacity to foresee reason-logic successes.

- Thinking without a sense of outcomes.
- No interest in outcomes, but only in the Now.
- Capacity to recognize the difference between order and disorder.
- Incapacity to recognize the difference between order and disorder.
- Assuming that disorder has REAL value to human survival. Failure to recognize motives until after the fact.
- Success in recognizing motives before the fact.
- Lack of educational courses called WISDOM 101.
- Lack of self-presence of WISDOM 101.
- No interest in wisdom, but only in achieving purposes and goals.
- Interest in wisdom.

33

IN ITS simple form, wisdom can be thought of as doing the right thing at the right time so that things turn out well, positive, and pro-survival.

To be sure, this also involves having some familiarity with whatever will end up producing negative results. However, not too much wisdom can emerge by focusing on what produces negative results. So, the onus, the obligation, the burden of wisdom is to focus on what will turn out well, positive, and pro-survival.

34

For reasons that are not entirely identifiable, during the nineteenth and twentieth centuries, the concept of the bad or negative was somehow transmuted into "what is wrong with US," and/or what is wrong with Mankind and Humanity.

It appears that finding out what was wrong (or bad) was at first a sociological endeavor that never culminated in much of anything. But the implications of what was wrong with us were soon incorporated into various psychologies, the arts, literature, drama, media, and fascinating entertainments, etc.

There was nothing essentially wrong with this, of course,

since it is necessary to learn about such negative matters. However, a significant side-effect that is hardly ever pointed up is that interest in what was right and good about US more or less disappeared into the black holes of what was wrong.

Indeed, as this humble book is being written, it is considered culturally and intellectually unfashionable to point up our US-species better, best, excellent, and often astonishing pro-good and pro-survival qualities, all of which still innately reside in human consciousness as such.

Focus, or too persistently much of it anyway, on what is wrong with us is probably a serious deterrent to wisdom-making. Who can expect to find evidence of wisdom among our species negative aspects and their manifesting activities, which are considered as existing because of the absence of it.

35

On average, wisdom is considered to consist of a last-ditch hope that will "save" us from what threatens us, after reason, logic, rationality, and gambling against the several morbid fates have failed.

But there is one other known definition that rarely appears in the available wisdom literature – to wit: Wisdom is what saves us from OURSELVES.

PART TWO

"...BEFORE WE DESTROY OURSELVES"

Chapter Seven

THE HYPNOTIC FASCINATION WITH FEAR, TERROR, WAR, ETC.

36

THE ASTRONOMER, Carl Sagan (1934-1996) is often quoted as saying: "Advanced civilizations, if they exist, aren't breaking their backs to save us before we destroy ourselves."

Sagan was probably speaking principally within the contexts of the ominous shadows cast by the Atomic/Nuclear Age that commenced when the first fission bomb was successfully tested at Alamogordo, New Mexico in 1945, and which types of bombs, as Weapons of Mass Destruction (WMDs), were thereafter increasingly improved upon and stockpiled by the greater nations, eventually including some lesser states. Stockpiling of such weapons throughout the world ultimately numbered at least in five-figure thousands upon thousands.

These clearly portend a gross and obscene over-kill potential, because detonating only ten or twenty of the larger and more refined weapons, together with their radioactive fallout, is more than enough to put a sterilizing end to life on Earth.

There was more to come. Sagan lived to see the stockpiling of high-kill biological WMDs, and so the fate of human consciousness is now doubly darkened by this additional ominous shadow.

37

Although the whole of the foregoing does represent a "bigger picture" of some kind, behind it is an even bigger one. As one way of putting it, this bigger picture has to do with what might be called the extent of human consciousness, out of which has inventively ascended the Age of WMDs, but which does NOT represent extensive human consciousness overall.

Rather, the Age of WMDs numbers as but ONE of the more miserable products of human consciousness, and which product is being tossed around within the bigger extent of it like a crap game.

There is, and always has been, MORE to human consciousness than using it merely to develop weaponry. Indeed, WMDs represent not consciousness, but "black holes" in it, into which are sucked innocent and guilty alike, all never to be seen again, even if some rotting, smoking, or glowing collateral damage is left behind.

Thus, there are at least two bigger pictures involved with all of this, the threatening destroy-ourselves one, and the other having to do with the fuller extent of human consciousness itself. For reasons that are all too immediate and obvious, the destroy-ourselves one is seen as the bigger, while the latter is seldom considered at all.

38

If one contemplates upon BOTH of these bigger pictures, it can eventually be realized that there is at least one great and ultra-important disparity between them.

Every fact and nuance that has led to the achievement of WMDs has been studied, scrutinized, researched, tested, developed, redeveloped, modulated, remodulated, refined, and super-refined in ways that are at least comparable to what goes into delicate brain surgery.

With respect to human consciousness and its real extent, however, there is an almost complete absence of anything comparable.

Furthermore, the development of what has led to the achieving of WMDs has enthusiastically proceeded along the lines of the no-holds-barred concept. Anything and everything, no matter what it was, needed to be included and examined so that the apex of the ultimate achievement could be brought into hand – i.e., the real extent of achieving the capability to destroy ourselves as a whole.

There are a number of reasons for this vacuum. But perhaps the most astonishing one has to do with the fact (well-known in some non-conventional categories of research) that various of the modern sciences, including that of psychology, elected to REJECT as being possible many phenomena of human consciousness even before they were inquired into and examined.

39

One way to conceptualize this disparity is to think in terms of dollar/manhours that have been devoted to research and building of WMDs, and to compare same that have been devoted to research and development of human consciousness.

During the last seven decades of the twentieth century, the development of WMDs was always surrounded by extreme secrecy, and so we shall never know the world's maximum expenditure toward achieving them. Based on some published figures, however, a conservative guesstimate lands us in the vicinity of at least 50,000 billion dollar/manhours. Compared to THIS, any dollar/manhours devoted to research and development of human consciousness equates to about a very small fraction of 1 cent.

Thus, there exists the great disparity between the extent of knowledge relevant to achieving WMDs, and the extent of knowledge relevant to human consciousness, which is nil enough to constitute a great gap or vacuum in, of all things, knowledge of our fuller selves. If one dares to hypothesize it, somewhere in the real extent of human consciousness there might exist the real capability of saving ourselves as a whole.

If not, then our only hope is the one the esteemed astronomer hinted at – the hope that "advanced civilizations" (i.e., extraterrestrials) might come down, intervene, and save us "before we destroy ourselves."

40

There arises the interesting question having to do with why advanced civilizations, if they exist, should be interested in a species-with-consciousness that devotes mountains of wealth and effort solely to achieve the capability of destroying itself.

From this there follows yet another interesting question. If advanced civilizations exist elsewhere, one really needs to set about wondering what has made them so "advanced."

Surely something along these lines would have to do with their research and development of their OWN forms of consciousness – at least to the degree that such development has taken them, at the very least, somewhat beyond massively destroying themselves before they could achieve the status of being "advanced."

This could only mean that THEY would have found and developed, in their consciousness, elements of collective life supporting factors that could have advanced them beyond the life-destroying stage in their own histories.

Some such collective life-supporting elements might even exist in our own species. But the very little we actually know, in our present conventional terms, of our own innate consciousness resembles little more than a few pebbles occasionally thrown into the great ocean of it.

Even so, some few have made some probes into that ocean, and thereby have sought to establish that there is more to our species consciousness than is generally appreciated, and which, furthermore, is usually vigorously denied and then laughed out of town.

Chapter Eight

THE "RAPTURE" ARCHETYPE

41

CARL SAGAN'S words are interesting from a number of perspectives.

The first has to do with whether he assumed the real existence of "advanced civilizations." Part of an answer here might be concluded in the positive, because he published a science-fiction novel entitled CONTACT, from which the famous movie of the same title was produced.

In the novel, the "contact" came about in a very strange manner via the initiative of the ETs who "sent down" a series of blueprints and instructions on how to build a spaceship-portal so that we could translate ourselves to them.

This gave Sagan the opportunity to dramatize his version of an "advanced civilization," which we do NOT find populated with little green men, greys, reptilians, androids, robots, intelligent machines, alien mind parasites, alien energy-sucking "vampires," or any form of lovable or dangerous monsters so fond to Earth-based peoples' imaginations.

Instead, his advanced civilization was not just "advanced" as we might think of it, but also extremely more "mature," and was composed of a collective composite of many altogether giving the impression of covering astronomical volumes of cosmic space.

Although elements of physicality are hinted at, the collectively advanced civilization is principally composed of shared and sharable consciousness in which even the concept of mind has receded to a diminished role. Within this linked consciousness, everything is "known," and our Earth-based distinctions between the Past, the NOW, and the Future have largely disappeared except for being points of consciousness focus.

42

Although Sagan did not express it as such, this more mature, advanced consciousness roughly equates to what, in evolving Earth-based terms, is being referred to as "reticulated consciousness."

RETICULATE refers to anything that resembles a net or network, specifically having veins, fibers, or lines crossing.

In genetics, it refers to whatever exhibits or constitutes evolutionary change dependent on complex new combinations of genes from varied strains of a diversified interbreeding population.

In recent advances at today's cutting edge of brain-mind-consciousness research, it refers to dividing, marking, or constructing so as to form a network, and/or, to distribute by a network that has become reticulated.

For clarity, this refers to neural nets in the brain and nervous systems innately capable of self-formatting evolutionary and complex new combinations in the brain, and thus within consciousness itself.

It can be mentioned that although the "mind" exhibits many functions (and an equal number of definitions), one of its most basic and recognizable characteristics is to function exclusively within limited and limiting sets of information packages and frames of reference whereby various "realities" are constructed at the individual and/or group-mental levels.

In Sagan's advanced consciousness civilizations, however, this mind limiting has been transcended, because he describes a vast reticulated consciousness in which there are no limits with respect to time, space, and energy, and even with respect to "knowing" what's in minds.

Considering all of the above, Sagan seems not only to have been an astronomer and a fiction writer, but also something of an intuitive "seer."

43

Sagan's words are also interesting from another perspective, albeit one that he may or may not have been aware of.

To get into this, it first needs to be pointed up that there are numerous hidden variables in the fuller extent of human consciousness that are "hidden" only because what we can call "conventional modern formats of consciousness" have, frankly speaking, refused to consider any possibility of their actual reality.

In Sagan's often quoted words, there are three nuances of meaning that are not being given the attention they deserve: (1) Advanced civilizations; (2) aren't saving us; (3) before we destroy ourselves. These three nuances are important to the larger contexts of this book, and they will often enter into the discussions ahead. So, we will briefly introduce them here.

At first, most attention and interest is quite likely to focus on the "advanced civilizations" part because if they exist then it can be hoped they will arrive, or come down, and save us. These "civilizations" of course refer to extraterrestrial ones elsewhere in the cosmos.

In comparison, little attention will be focused on the "destroy ourselves" part, perhaps because our species has a long history of such, and so it is taken for granted that we will somehow wreck upon ourselves the Ultimate Big Destruction.

The "aren't saving us" part obviously reflects something of Sagan's disappointment that the "saving us" part has not yet taken place.

44

With all due respect for Sagan's three nuances, the second one refers to a hope that we could be saved from our own destruction by more advanced elements than we, so far, have in hand.

This "hope to be saved" has two Earth-based names, the first of which is traditional, apparently of great antiquity, and quite familiar – SALVATION.

In English, this term has two established definitions: (1) the saving of man from the power and effects of sin [of which the conduct of destruction is one]; and (2) liberation from clinging to the phenomenal world of appearances and the achieving of union with ultimate reality.

This "ultimate reality" also has a traditional name dating from antiquity: PARADISE – "a place of bliss, felicity, or delight [in which destruction or threat of it is absent]."

45

The "hope to be saved" also has another tern of reference, RAPTURE, which, in older English, was defined as: (1) the act of conveying a person from one place to another, especially to a utopia or to heaven; and (2) transport of mind, mental exaltation, or absorption, especially via ecstasy and joy [in which the ominous threat of destruction is also absent].

The "hope to be saved" from our own self-destruction by intervention of "advanced civilizations" clearly reflects the rapture archetype that has made its appearance time and again in our history, usually in the presence of great social or natural threats that seem irresolvable.

46

An ARCHETYPE is defined as "the original pattern or model of which all things of the same type are representations or copies."

By itself, this definition, seems mundane enough. But it achieved enormous limelight when the great intuitive psychologist, Carl Gustav Jung (1875-1961), proposed and demonstrated that archetypes of numerous kinds exist within the collective unconscious of humanity.

Jung's impressive book entitled THE ARCHETYPES OF THE COLLECTIVE UNCONSCIOUS first published in 1959 is a bit of a challenge to work though. But he explains that the concept of the unconscious was, at first, thought of as being limited to denoting the state of repressed or forgotten contents (memories).

The OTHER great psychologist of the time, Sigmund Freud (1856-1939), agreed that the unconscious was nothing more than the gathering place of forgotten and repressed contents. For

Freud, the unconscious was of an exclusively personal (individual) nature, although he was aware of its archaic and mythological thought forms.

47

Jung went one step further. He indicated that a more or less superficial layer of the unconscious is undoubtedly personal, and this he referred to as the "personal unconscious." However, this personal unconscious rests upon a deeper layer, which does not derive from personal experience and is not a personal acquisition but is inborn.

He called this deeper layer the "collective" unconscious, because the term "collective" refers to a part of the unconscious that is not individual but universal.

He discusses (at some great length and in several of his volumes) that archetypes of the collective unconscious appear in dreams, visions, myths, and fairytales, etc., perhaps via specific but similar cultural "stamps," which have been handed down via the collective unconscious through long periods of time.

48

Some archetypes are easier to recognize than others: for instance, the mother-goddess, the seductive feminine Venus, the masculine Mars, the overdeveloped Eros, cult-heroes, the maternal element, forms of Rebirth, the Savior archetype, the old bearded man of Wisdom, and various archetypes of Transformation – all of which are universally present and have always been alluringly and charismatically responded to throughout the human world.

49

One of the tough points about collective archetypes is that IF they innately exist, then some kind of really deep "species memory" is required.

Many pre-modern societies did not have much of a problem with respect to this. But it did become one during the buildup of modern scientific times during which it was conceptualized that the individual was entirely discrete within Self, had no innate links to anything else, and as such could not somewhere within Self have anything like deeply buried species-collective memory.

Indeed, Jung's concept of collective archetypes at first faced a rather rocky road in this regard, although appreciation of at least some of the archetypes has slowly been accepted during the last forty years.

50

As with all other of the archetypes, the existence of the rapture archetype would have to be based in an "original pattern or model of which all things [thereafter] of the same type are representations or copies."

The rapture archetype thus requires two original patterns or models that became deeply imprinted in the collective unconscious memory: (1) the advent of some nearing colossal calamity that could not be gotten out of the way of, except (2) by the arrival from elsewhere of transport that could literally lift off or extract those in danger of being obliterated by the calamity.

Thereby saving them - much, it might be understood, to their ecstatic and rapturous relief, after which anything elsewhere might be thought of as paradise, utopian, or heavenly. Being "saved" by such automatically implies the chance to start again.

All of this might be laughed at, and skeptics might insist that nothing of the kind really happened. Even so, the rapture archetype theme has importantly run through human history as an expectant river of fresh water, both in fact, myth, and fiction. Even Moses "lifted" the Jews out of Egypt, leading them to their homeland.

The archetype sometimes even has a reverse vector to it, for the British once got the idea of sending most of their criminals to Australia simply to ease overcrowding in their prisons, and which country was soon seen, by the former criminals, as a new paradise plus a chance to start again.

The rapture archetype is often seized upon for fictional purposes of entertainment, more recently, for examples, in tales of the fabled Shangri-La, in episodes of the several Star Trek series, and in movies in which helicopters arrive to extract those who find themselves in terminal danger.

And even today, as this book is being pieced together, if

there was an option to go elsewhere to escape the otherwise senseless threats of weapons of mass destruction, you can bet your bottom dollar that there would quickly be a wholesale migration to that elsewhere no matter where –thereby leaving the fulminators and factotums of WMDs to suffer, in the darkening shadows of their non-wisdom, their own self-imposed doom.

Chapter Nine

THE ARCHETYPAL FEAR OF CALAMITOUS DESTRUCTION

51

OF COURSE, the question now emerges as to whether the original elements of the rapture archetype ever really did occur in a scope large enough  to imprint into the permanent collective unconscious of the human species.

There was one voice in the wilderness of all of this that said 'Yes," at least with respect to a probable gigantic calamity that occurred in the very distant past.

This was the voice of Immanuel Velikovsky (1895-1979), born in Russia, worked in Palestine, and ultimately in the United States. He studied natural sciences at the University of Edinburgh, then history, humanities, and medicine in Moscow, biology in Berlin, the workings of the brain in Zurich, and psychoanalysis in Vienna.

An early article entitled "On the Energetic of the Psyche" earned him the respect and confidence of Freud, and of the once equally famous Swiss neurologist and psychiatrist, Eugen Bleuler (1857-1939), and his expertise became so appreciated that many psychiatric professionals sent to him their hard-to-crack psychoanalytic cases.

Thus, Velikovsky's career loomed large and positive ahead of him. However, he had always taken deep interest in how and why deep traumas and other effects could be found in the human PSYCHE, which is defined in modern psychiatry as follows: "The psyche, like other organs, possesses its own form and function, its embryology, gross and microscopic anatomy, physiology and pathology."

Otherwise, the term is taken from ancient Greek and Sanskrit terms referring to the PROCESSES of "breath, to breathe, to blow, to give or to stimulate into life." Sadly, and somewhat missing the mark, these ancient definitions are rendered into modern English as "soul or spirit" and later as "mind," which are commonly thought of things, or at least as entities, and not as life-giving processes.

Freud was the first to attempt a comprehensive schematization of the psyche, describing it "as consisting in general as having the conscious and the unconscious divisions, each of which is made up of a great number of compartments."

Specifying the "mind-psyche," Freud indicated that, like all other organs of the body, it has its own local functions and those functions that are intimately associated with adjacent and distant organs. It is like the cardiovascular system in that it reaches all parts of the body; "it also serves to adjust the total organism to the needs or demands of the environment."

Not wanting to put words in the venerable Freud's mouth, whether of breath, soul, spirit, or mind, it seems like he was referring to what is now being termed the interacting networks of "reticulated consciousness" (earlier mentioned), which have their "conscious and unconscious divisions."

52

Among psychoanalytic traumas was the "deep" fear of tremendous cataclysms that often came to the surface in his patients, but the sources of which they could not otherwise have actually experienced. So, the sources of such traumas were to be found in the unconscious division of the psyche.

But here was a great archetypal theme that Velikovsky was probably familiar with, in that such cataclysms were often portrayed in the myths of premodern societies, in the dramatic arts of antiquity and later, and even in painterly examples of certain artists. As but one well-known example of this, the post renaissance British artist, John Martin (1789-1854) produced several monumental paintings that can hardly be mistaken for anything else than Earth in gigantic upheaval.

53

It seems that Velikovsky concluded that gigantic cataclysms had happened and that unconscious memory of them was somehow deeply buried in the psyche and in the collective unconscious of the human race as well.

He soon published what was to become a series of books, the first entitled WORLDS IN COLLISION (1950), in which he proposed, and gave considerable evidence for, his contention that more than once within prehistoric and historic times the orbits of the planets of our solar system were disrupted and ran amok and caused enormous cataclysms. He drew his evidence from excavated history, from ancient texts, folklore, and the sacred writings of peoples over the globe.

54

With the publication of this book, Velikovsky's reputation thereafter and until his death found itself in deep, very deep, do-do, the kindest expression of which was that he "kindled a worldwide debate," which was conducted not only with enormous fervor, but also with serious dollops of malice, vengeful mouth-frothing by energetic intellectuals, etc.

The central reason for the debate was that when he published his first and other books, for example, EARTH IN UPHEAVAL (1955), cosmologists and astronomers were still much wedded to the idea that cosmic changes, when and if they took place, did so not suddenly but only very slowly.

Otherwise the cosmos was governed not by "ages of chaos," but by something at least similar to the doctrine of cosmic uniformitarianism – the concept "that existing processes acting in the same manner as can be seen in the present are sufficient to account for all changes."

55

Since Velikovsky's death in 1979, cosmologists and astrophysicists have had several occasions to revise those older estimations of his work, and even, in some cases, to quietly retire them.

It is now understood that centers of galaxies often explode, sending forth powerful wave fronts that can ultimately, and without warning, impact and disrupt planetary star systems and even distant galaxies. Black holes can form, and suck into them everything in their expansive proximity. In other words, the cosmos can experience ages of chaos.

There also remains the question of the asteroid belt between Mars and Jupiter, which was either (1) slowly formed or (2) suddenly came into existence. The total mass of all of the asteroids in the belt is sufficient enough to have once formed a planet much larger than Earth, perhaps even equal to the massive size of Jupiter. If not formed slowly by some kind of cosmic force, then the only other answer is that it somehow exploded or was rendered into chunks by some kind of collision with a celestial object large enough to demolish it.

What is known for sure is that most of the documented meteors and/or ice chunks called comets have originated from the asteroid belt. It is now accepted that one large such chunk did impact Earth, and thereby destroyed the age of dinosaurs, including thousands of other species. How's that for an age of chaos?

And as well, during 2001 and 2002, Earth has experienced a few significantly near misses by wandering meteorites that have neither been documented before nor expected.

56

But Velikovsky's voice was still to be heard from his grave. His book MANKIND IN AMNESIA (1982), published posthumously, addressed the existence of collectively innate memory of the human race, in which his "theory of cosmic catastrophism finds its psychological counterpart."

In this book, he enlarges upon details of his theory of "a collective amnesia" (first broached in WORLDS IN COLLISION). This theory was his first attempt "to explain the inability of people to look at the overwhelming evidence of global catastrophes that is unequivocally in existence, and the unwillingness to see the implications of that evidence."

As he explained, "The memory of the cataclysms was erased, not because of lack of written traditions, but because of some characteristic process that later caused entire nations, together with their literate men [to substitute] allegories or metaphors where actual cosmic disturbances were clearly described."

What he more clearly meant was that the actual, and obviously horrific, disturbances were suppressed into the collective unconscious, and that the actual cataclysms were reinterpreted via less ominous, less fear rendering, and more amenable allegories and metaphors.

This "characteristic" is quite well understood in psychology, or at least the functional dynamics of it are, for people cannot consciously live with chronic fear of the past. So, whatever is involved gradually subsides into the individual subconscious.

But if the fear has been collectively universal and species-wide enough, it subsides as a collective "worlds in destruction" archetype into in the collective unconscious, thus ending up as a species psychological kind of amnesia.

Even if deeply buried in the unconscious division of the human psyche, anything encountered that is suggestive of or similar to the original shared experience can cause the suppressed unconscious memories of it to emotionally rumble around.

Thus, Velikovsky can be considered as dissecting the first half of the rapture archetype, the collective unconscious memory of threat of unavoidable destruction, or at least the threat of destruction out of control. By itself, the "worlds in destruction" archetype leaves one with a sense of gloom and doom.

The second half of the rapture archetype (to be discussed in pages ahead) is based on being saved, via some extraordinary means, specifically by being lifted away or extracted from the unavoidable destruction, and which Carl Sagan was disappointed had not already occurred during his lifetime.

Chapter Ten

"IN FEAR AND TREMBLING"

57

CERTAIN INTREPID individuals say they climb precipitous mountains because they are "THERE" (i.e., there to be climbed).

In a similar sense, it could be said that weapons of mass destruction (WMDs) have come about because their inventors say they are "there" to be invented.

However, if the history of the development of WMDs is slowly studied in detail, it seems that such weapons have been invented and developed majorly because of fear that if "we" don't then someone else will.

Equally present is the fear that if others have developed them, then "we" must also have them, if only for purposes of equal deterrence via equal powers of mass destruction.

From this particular perspective, it seems that the extensive proliferation of fearsome WMDs have come about to equalize the FEAR potentials among those who have them in hand, or at least to equally distribute ominous apprehensions with respect to their eventual use.

Available records show that this FEAR potential is so significant and so great that it overwhelmed the concerns of many who could intuit or foresee the probable Final Outcome of WMDs.

Thus, the whole of this is seen as logical and rational, at least among the higher echelons of those who manage equal fear deterrence.

58

The only remaining problem has to do with matching and becoming equal with any new WMDs that can arise anywhere there is sufficient expertise to take WMDs to their next higher and more massive destructive potentials.

Indeed, already underway here and there:

Development of neutron bombs, E-bombs, sonic bombs, EM pulse bombs, X-ray emitting bombs;

Various kinds of space-orbiting energy "guns" that boil brains and/or sterilize males in broad targeted land-surface areas;

Biological genetic engineering of hereto unknown mass-killer diseases;

Certain chemical compounds that interfere with and retard human nervous systems, sexual proficiency, and sense of directions;

Other chemical compounds that artificially magnify the emotions of fear, hatred, anger, and rage.

Etc., etc., etc., and so forth ad infinitum, because many behind-the-scenes experts say that the Age of WMDs is yet only in its infancy. All of these forthcoming developments are very trendy within WMD circles, and in all nations.

So, where Oh where are the advanced civilizations that might save us from our own destructions, and WHEN oh WHEN will they arrive?

59

In MANKIND IN AMNESIA, Velikovsky undertook to expand on his theory of repressed collective memories of many cosmic catastrophes that befell our ancestors, the most recent of which, in his time-line, occurred only about a hundred generations ago.

As reviewed in the book's Foreword (by Lynn E. Rose, professor of philosophy at State University of New York at Buffalo), Velikovsky sought to give evidence which, if openly examined, shows that "Virtually every aspect of human behavior, every pattern in human history, and every article of human belief . . . [every] human thought and action have been [unconsciously] shaped and molded by repressed collective memories of cosmic catastrophes."

60

For helpful clarity here, it must be reminded that Velikovsky was, in essence, not talking of the catastrophes themselves, but of collective human "race" (i.e., species) memories of them repressed into the collective unconscious division of the human psyche.

These memories had become collectively imprinted into the innate unconscious division and thus forwarded onward through succeeding generations as innately inherited memory - in the same way that all archetypes are, as discussed by Carl G. Jung in his books dealing with the archetypes of the collective unconscious.

More specifically, however, Velikovsky did not principally focus on the memories themselves, but the emotions of fear induced by them, and "copies" of which became imprinted, contained, and perpetuated through the collective unconscious.

61

It must be admitted that there are many different kinds of psychological and emotional fear, each of which has its different experiential source. It must also be admitted that fear does have a scale that ranges from slight, important, significant, and up to and including overwhelming kinds of it.

Thus, if our ancestors did experience global catastrophes, it must again be admitted that FEAR engendered by these would fit into the big-time overwhelming category, at least with respect to consciousness of those who survived to repopulate in the post-catastrophe years.

62

Before continuing with Velikovsky, it is worthwhile making a brief aside to consider new evidence of global catastrophe set forth in a recent book entitled EARTH UNDER FIRE (1997) by Paul LaViolette. Subtitled "Humanity's Survival of the Apocalypse," he reviews, among several other mind-boggling factors, the now increasingly accepted astronomical fact that the centers of galaxies occasionally "explode."

Before they again calm down, the explosions successively emanate a series of intense high-energy, and very destructive, "superwave-fronts" (i.e., superwave event horizons) that eventually expand to distances beyond the galaxy edge itself, sometimes triggering certain stars to go supernova.

Such superwave-fronts not only have their own enormous destructive actions, but when they meet with stars (or suns) local within the galaxy, those stellar bodies also go superactive, sending out copious amounts of their own deadly radiations.

LaViolette is not talking simply through his own hat, for he depends on and quotes from a vast array of published scientific astronomic papers that deal with the nature of exploding galaxies.

Earth's participation in superwave fronts can be confirmed by geological evidence, but the methods involved are very detailed and beyond the scope of this book.

63

According to published scientific documents, it appears that the center of our own Milk/ Way galaxy underwent such a super explosion at about 36,000 B.C., with at least one of its superwave event horizons reaching Earth at approximately 12,160 B.C., well within the memory of surviving pre-Flood peoples global-wide.

Within this particular event, our local Sun also went superactive, scalding Earth with yet another source of radiation destructivity. Earth was still under enormous glaciation at the time, and so this event probably caused rapid, if not instantaneous, melting of vast flooding of broken ice and meltwaters. LaViolette's description of what probably happened on Earth, horrific enough, is quite detailed, and again depends on scientific evidence, but also on cultural narratives of it.

To shorten the description of this cataclysm, LaViolette quotes what might be an allegorical memory of it found in the Second Epistle of Saint Peter (3:10): "But the day of the Lord will come as a thief in the night; in which the heavens shall pass away with a great noise, and the elements shall melt with fervent heat, the earth also and the works that are therein shall be burned up."

While these cosmic superwave event horizons may not be

the same as the catastrophes Velikovsky had in mind, both are clearly in the same cosmic category.

64

In MANKIND IN AMNESIA, Velikovsky reiterates some of his earlier thinking about the existence of a collective mind in the early stages of the development of the species. He indicated that individualization (i.e., separate organisms or individuals) accompanies the evolution from lower to higher forms, yet the collective mind is never fully erased in man; it comes to the fore in excited states of mind, also in crowds swept by emotions.

He thought that if this aspect were fully studied, it would be seen that the autonomy of the mental domains of separate individuals must have early developed as a more complicated and higher state within the origins of our species.

He then goes on to point up that the early concept of telepathy as an archaic form of emotional thought transmission still exists within the collective mind of our species. Therefore, the archaic form of telepathy also innately remains in the unconscious collective mind, in the same way that all archaic categories do.

This archaic form of telepathy might not undergo conscious development in individuals, but it still remains in the collective unconscious where it continues to exist and react as a non-conscious responsive source of "reciprocal influence" within all individuals of the species.

By this, he meant that a reciprocating influence is mutually corresponding and is transmitted, shared, or experienced in common by each individual.

65

Velikovsky then went on to discuss some of the results of the archaic fear deeply embedded within the collective unconscious that became imprinted, as archetypes, because of sudden and tremendous cataclysms, which induced a collective "frightened state of mind" in the survivors.

Such survivors obviously would have had "fear and trembling" that such might come again, accompanied by two fervent hopes – that they would not, or that the people would somehow be saved from them if they did reoccur.

Velikovsky assumed that the very ancient sages and their peoples lived in a frightened state of mind for some time, "justified by the events they or their close ancestors had witnessed."

As time went on, that fear, always knocking at the apprehensive door, together with the hope that the cataclysms would not reoccur, "degenerated into the worship" and appeasement of planetary and other deities, resulting in religio-political wars and conflicting superstitions, which thereafter held sway for several millennia – and much of which still goes on today.

66

Velikovsky pointed up that in more modern times, the whole of this ancient fear and trembling was assuaged, among intellectuals at least, by "a dogmatic belief" in the hypothesis of uniformitarianism raised to the status of fundamental law based on the premise that no cataclysmic event ever took place on the planet, and so could not have had a part in shaping the mental life of people on it.

He hypothesized that the long adherence, in various forms, to the dogma of uniformitarianism was a "symptom of an all-embracing fear" of facing, and rationalizing away, the great past destructions, or even facing the historically documented experiences of our progenitors, as recent as eighty generations ago.

It is to be noted that the dogma of uniformitarianism underwent challenge only during the twentieth century when it was confirmed that great geological changes have taken place, great ocean-filling floods have also taken place, and, more recently, that exploding galaxy events also happen. This is to say that although things can remain uniformitarian for periods of time, there nonetheless do occur non-uniformitarian epochs of calamitous change.

Chapter Eleven

"WHY WAR?" AND WHY PEACE DISAPPEARS

67

SOMEWHAT prophetically, it seems, chapter 5 of MANKIND IN AMNESIA is entitled "The Age of Terror," and its first subsection posits the thematic question of "Why War?" I.e., why ARE there wars, why do they come about?

Velikovsky begins by recounting an exchange of letters between Albert Einstein and Sigmund Freud. Einstein, the physicist and pacifist wrote to Freud, then the world's leading psychoanalyst, asking whether the fields of "psychiatry and psychoanalysis knows [of] a panacea against the slaughter of human beings organized in states, [justified by] a sanctioned destruction of human life."

Einstein indicated that "It would be of the greatest service to us all were you to present the problem of world peace in the light of your recent discoveries, for such a presentation might blaze the trail for new and fruitful modes of action."

In his reply, Freud indicated that he visualized "no likelihood of our being able to suppress humanity's aggressive tendencies" – a gloomy prognosis, indeed.

68

When the gist of the Einstein-Freud exchange on this matter became broadly known, it seems to have inspired, in 1935, over three hundred psychiatrists from thirty nations to sign a manifesto on "war prevention."

In the manifesto, and at variance with Freud's ominous

prognosis, the signatories stated: "We psychiatrists declare that our science is sufficiently advanced for us to distinguish between, real, pretended, and unconscious motives, even in statesmen."

Following this, a large congress of psychologists convened in Paris in 1937. The keynote address, read by a Professor Claparede of Geneva, was entitled "Hatred among the Nations," which, in Velikovsky's view, did not dissect the sources of the "Hatred," but only "contained pious hopes and expressions of faith in human progress."

The efforts of the 1935 manifesto and in the 1937 Paris conference amounted to little more than pissing into the wind, for the horrors of World War II and its Holocaust was launched in 1939, quickly followed by escalating atomic bomb developments, the wars in Korea and Indochina, etc., etc., etc.

Thereafter, little was heard of possible psychiatric and psychological contributions that might contribute to war avoidance, but there did occur commentary that psychological study for the basis of war was not only "futile" but also "impotent."

69

Velikovsky (bless his much unjustly maligned heart) took umbrage against the impotency of "psychologists to find and expose the roots of the scourge known as war" – principally because "The idea that wars begin in the minds of men, and that it is in the minds of men that defenses of peace must be constructed, is as old as the history of relations between organized societies."

By his use of "the minds of men," he was not just referring to the conscious mind, but to the totality of it that includes not only the "private [individual] subconscious," but also the division of the fundamental "archaic" psyche – the collective unconscious which contains the suppressed contents of the innate species mind entire.

70

Velikovsky seems to have been appreciative of the works of

Carl G. Jung (earlier discussed), who brought the existence of the collective unconscious into great luminosity, together with its many main archetypes that are identical in all humanity, although perhaps aesthetically expressed a little differently in various cultures.

Velikovsky points up, however, that it did not occur to Jung that common and terrifying experiences, in which all participated and from which few survived, were also "engraved in man's inheritable substance" of the collective unconscious, and which engraving carries the imprints of the awesome terror and fear that would have been a full part of the cataclysmic experience, the whole of which would have been suppressed into mankind's amnesia as fear-terror archetypes always tremulously waiting on the indistinct edges of psychological consciousness.

71

Summarizing together several of Velikovsky's thoughts along these lines (and perhaps putting some words into his mouth), he maintained that although the biggest and most spectacular fear archetypes have actual experiential sources in the distant past, they are unconsciously maintained forward, in the collective unconscious, into the future by fears that something akin to the initial experiences will happen again.

He insists that, in keeping with all psychological suppressing, the suppression into the collective unconscious was, in the first instance, the need to forget the fear-terror, but a forgetting that is always connected to the hope that reasons for the fear-terror will not have possible repetitions.

It is for this double psychological reason that the fear archetypes are always present on the indistinct edges of psychological consciousness.

72

Meanwhile, always verging on consciousness of them, through the ages, the sources of the fear-terrors can be worshiped as "gods" in order to propitiate or placate the sources (of this he gives many historical examples), or the fear-terror archetypes can stimulate "the urge to emulate them."

That is, literally, but unconsciously, reenact fear-terror via the "minds" of those who fall victim to the fear-terror archetypes (of which he also gives many historical examples).

Thus, such situations are a basic cause of the "aggressive tendencies" of war ("the recurrent scourge") having then psychological beginning in "minds of men."

PART THREE

IS HUMAN CONSCIOUSNESS "BIGGER" THAN FEAR, TERROR, WAR, ETC.?

Chapter Twelve

THE POLARIZATION OF FEAR vs WISDOM

73

EVEN IF the concept of the collective unconscious (and its powerful archetypes) might not be thought of as pertinent, it must be observed that our species is overly preoccupied and fascinated by the topics of war, fear, violence, etc., whether real or imagined.

This preoccupation and fascination even extends into fictional tales via comic books, novels, and movies whereby readers and viewers can thrill to and vicariously experience fear, war, and especially great science-fiction destructions on a cosmic scale (for example, War of the Worlds, When Worlds Collide, and Armageddon types, etc.).

Such fictions are brought out by entrepreneurs of the entertainment arts who may or may not have read the works of Jung, Velikovsky, or others, but who have otherwise discovered the large sales potential of such productions.

At any rate, fear is a big-time element in human consciousness, and has been such within at least historical memory, for even ancient myths can be seen to incorporate it, as well as passing it, via the myths, into the future.

74

In our more modern times, FEAR has been rather briefly defined as "An unpleasant often strong emotion caused by anticipation or awareness of danger" – which is to say, defined as an emotion.

However, the meanings of term that entered English at about 1175 were taken from Old English, Old Saxon, and Middle High German words that might have been based on the Aryan root PER meaning "to go through" sudden calamity, terrible dangers, events, and perils. In the sense of these early renderings, FEAR did not have an explicit psychological context, but more pointedly referred to actually experiencing (going through) something sudden and really awful.

It wasn't until about 1490 that the term began to include "to regard with reverence and awe, to revere," and it wasn't until somewhere between about 1515-1590 that the term became psychologically "personified," i.e., referring to emotions of individuals having a fear-like apprehension "of some future evil" before it occurs. As will be discussed later, having apprehensions of danger before they come about falls within the scope of fore-seeing or fore-sensing, elements of which are workhorses within the contexts of wisdom.

75

Fear has always played an over-large role throughout written human history, and in pre-history, too, throughout which fear-sagas were forwarded via oral traditions in all cultures.

It is therefore surprising that the topic of fear, as a major human component of our species entire, has not been given much philosophical consideration. At least there is no major entry for it in the otherwise all-inclusive ENCYCLOPEDIA OF PHILOSOPHY (in eight volumes) published in 1967, edited by Paul Edwards, and which covers some 2,000 years of philosophical discourse. Fear is mentioned only twice in the Index – in association with death and tragedy.

This considerable omission, one can suppose, is more than just mysterious, being neigh on inexplicable. After all, it is quite obvious that FEAR, or fear of it, has always constituted one of the major "drives" of the collective consciousness of our species – as well as our collective unconscious.

76

There IS an entry for FEAR in the PSYCHIATRIC DICTIONARY

(Fifth Edition, Robert Campbell, Ed., 1981). This is not an off-beat dictionary, but the fifth edition of a completely conventionally accepted one. From it we can learn that there are at least three major types of fear.

The first of these is the "guilt-fear," the fear that dire consequences are in store for one because of having committed a misdeed, or for experiencing a forbidden impulse, or, worse, for indulging in it.

Second, is the fear-impulse, defined as "a fear that arises within the individual(s), more or less directly from an instinctual source," i.e., a source that has become innate within the collective unconscious. In another entry, the fear-impulses are referred to as PHYLOGENETIC MNEMES defined as "The racial ancestral memory preset in the deep unconscious of the individual."

Third, we learn that REAL FEAR is in contrast to "fear-impulse," in that the former "is associated with some real object [or situation] in the environment."

After mentioning these three fears, an A to Z list of some 218 "Fear of" topics are listed, but which are referred to as PHOBIAS and defined as: "Morbid fear associated with morbid anxiety." Did you get that?

Well, in its first instance, MORBID refers to "of, relating to, or characteristic of disease; grisly, gruesome." But in psychiatric and psychological contexts it refers to "abnormally susceptible to, or characterized by, gloomy or unwholesome feelings."

Among many other morbid phobias, the lengthy list of "fear-of' includes fear of: anything new, bad men, bees, being touched, brain disease, contamination, corpses, darkness; also fear-of everything (panophobia), demons, dogs, failure, female genitals; also fear-of flying, hell, parasites, people, pleasure, rectal excreta, ridicule, semen, solitude, tapeworms, vomiting, water, women, and work, etc.

It can be noted that several other well-known phobias did not make it onto the list: for example, fear of courage, denial, erectile muscles, intersexuality, males, money, poverty, rejection, and war.

The A to Z list can be broken apart into categories, one of them consisting of: phobias having to do with colors, comets, dawn, daylight, electricity, flash, floods, gravity, heaven (uranophobia), heredity, ideas, infinity, innovation, large objects, lightening, meteors, mind, missiles, motion, myths, northern lights, open space, rain, red, sacred things, stars, sunlight, thunder, and trembling, etc.

When these fears (or phobias) are experienced, they do seem to resemble super-fears in the collective unconscious that are similar to many of Velikovsky's concepts of "archaic" fears.

Please note that "uranophobia" is related to "uranography," which is a science dealing with the description of the heavens and the celestial bodies i.e., astronomy.

The topic of wisdom is not mentioned in the PSYCHIATRIC DICTIONARY, perhaps because it is not characterized by morbid disease, perhaps because it is outside of or beyond the psychiatric worldview, or, for that matter, beyond the modern West's psychological worldview.

77

The term WISDOM is found in most dictionaries, even in the extremely inefficient WORLD BOOK DICTIONARY (1979), in which it is vacuously defined as "knowledge and good judgment based on experience." Indeed, as is rather broadly known, many can accumulate a lot of knowledge and experience, but not make contact with wisdom, or even with common sense.

Better dictionaries, such as Webster's Seventh New Collegiate (1969), contribute a bit more, or at least help establish a slightly bigger picture of it.

Therein, WISDOM is defined as:
   a. Accumulated philosophic and scientific learning – knowledge;
   b. Ability to discern inner qualities and relationships – insight;
   c. Good sense – judgment;
   d. A wise attitude or course of action – prediction;
   e. The teachings of the ancient men – sages.
   f. It turns out, however, that the philosophic encyclopedia mentioned earlier (the one that did not have an entry for "fear") DOES have an entry for WISDOM, and a rather extensive one at that. It begins:

g. "WISDOM in its broadest and commonest sense denotes sound and serene judgment regarding the conduct of life. It may be accompanied by a broad range of knowledge, by intellectual acuteness, and by speculative depth, but it is not to be identified with any of these and may appear in their absence. It involves intellectual grasp or insight, but it is concerned not so much with the ascertainment of fact or the elaboration of theories as with the means and ends of practical life."

78

There is one important word in the above quotation that many might slip past without realizing its fuller significance with respect either to fear or to wisdom.

That word is SERENE, defined in most modern dictionaries as: "Clear and free of storms or unpleasant change; marked by utter calm; tranquility; serenity."

It doesn't take too much imagination to think that FEAR and SERENITY are at opposite ends of the universe, so to speak, in that fear, if it is ominous and potent enough, could seriously deteriorate and wreck grips on knowledge, insight, judgment, and contacts with "inner" qualities associated with the emergence of wisdom.

The term POLARITY refers to "diametrical opposition," and "the particular state either positive or negative with respect to the two poles or to electrification" that repel each other.

These definitions can be translated into fear-versus-wisdom contexts, in that fear not only reflects a negative state, but also in that the emotion-impulses of fear can become so highly charged that they overwhelm all other aspects of a positive state otherwise available in innate human consciousness.

FEAR _ _ _ WISDOM
(polarized)

It is easy enough to understand that fear impulses, if great enough (as in terror, even threat of it), can seriously interrupt all other categories of human consciousness, totally wrecking the serenity category – which sends any wisdom and its components down the tubes. If fear impulses are big enough, then wisdom potentials can increasingly diminish to the blotto vanishing point.

79

Before his death, the controversial German philosopher, Friedrich Nietzsche (1844-1900), predicted that the twentieth century would be the bloodiest, most war-torn century ever.

His foresight was a resounding super-success, including extremes of deplorable destructions and inculcated terror-fear that even he could not have foreseen.

Indeed, some latter-day analysts theorize that the total extent of the twentieth century destructions was at least equal to all similar destructions inclusive of the last thousand years. In other words, one mere century of Big Time destructions, together with the still prevailing fears they engendered – now enhanced even more, of course, by the ominous proliferation of WMDs.

All of this is more or less acknowledged now. But there was one by-product of it that has hardly been recognized and pointed up.

As the actual and anticipated war fears and accompanying psychological disorientations of them mounted and increased, interest in and even discussion of, wisdom underwent an almost vertical decline, more or less like a precious gem thrown into the depths of a turbulent ocean. By at least the mid-1980s, even mention of the word was considered unfashionable among intellectuals, and it seems, according to publishing gossip, that publishers avoided the topic altogether, because such books would not sell.

In other words, the topic of wisdom underwent cultural rejection, largely, it was superficially thought, because it had failed to ameliorate the deepest do-do of continuing dread, fear, terrors, and potentials of future of wars, etc.

But there may be a more profound psychological reason, having to do with simple embarrassment that Great Mankind, otherwise possessed of mind, intelligence, insight, and knowledge, had collectively failed to enhance its indwelling wisdom category.

It can be speculated that warmongers, terror-purveyors, and

enthusiastic producers of WMDs, etc., have no need of wisdom, too much of which would be inconvenient and bothersome.

Thus, we hope for and await advanced civilizations to not only save us from ourselves, but also from our history of fear – because we do implicitly think that an advanced civilization would have done something about the fear category so as to become "advanced" rather than terminally self-destroying.

Chapter Thirteen

THE HA-HA QUESTION OF SERENITY

80

AS THE GROSS events and anxieties of the twentieth century took place and increased, it seems, in general, that experiencing serenity became something of a laughing matter.

It may be that some could experience it, if only for very short periods. But on the whole, large segments of people just about everywhere (in Asia, the modern West Europe and U.S.A., Siberia-Russia, Africa, Tibet, etc.) increasingly fell under such stresses that the sole goal was simply to get through the working day.

It is understandable that as conscious, subconscious, and unconscious fear-based anxieties increase through broad populations, the incidence of experiencing serenity must decline proportionately. Even if some do manage to experience serenity, most know it is only temporary.

Not surprisingly, there arose during the last three decades of the twentieth century an increasingly larger proliferation of self-help and guided instructional courses aimed at stress-anxiety coping and reduction, together with a smaller counterpart aimed at restoring if not serenity itself, at least a sense of it. The proliferation of such courses clearly attests to the fact that vast numbers of peoples had lost touch with serenity.

Certainty about what serenity WAS also became lost, or at least questionable, and something of a giggle factor as well. Serenity?

You've got to be joking. All one wants is to get through the difficulties, upsets, and potential horrors of the day without being totally wrecked.

81

Beyond the obvious factors mentioned above, there is another that, if spotted, is both strange and significant. It seems that in-depth discussions on the nature of serenity are few and far between, at least in the English language. Even definitions of the term are minimal, but they are worth examining here.

The origin of the word SERENE is uncertain, maybe taken from Old High German or Old French, or from a Greek term meaning "to become dry."

Entering English at about 1530 or earlier, SERENE as an adjective or verb, and SERENITY as a noun, referred to clear, fair, and calm weather, and to clearness and stillness of air and sky.

At about 1599, there was added the context of "Cheerful tranquility of mind, temper, countenance, etc."

In 1635, the term could also refer to "Cheerful tranquility, peacefulness of conditions, sometimes with express reference to sense," i.e., making calm, clear sense of things.

All definitions since these early three were reiterations of them – which signifies that little Western interest in serenity has taken place during the intervening six hundred years.

Yet serenity, if it takes place at all, can be thought of as an aspect of human consciousness per se, a seemingly important one at that, and one that most would like to have more of.

82

The situation was not the same in ancient Asia, however, in that at least THREE prominent kinds of serenity were identified, nurtured, and reinforced not only by extending knowledge, but actual experience of them.

It must be established that ancient Asian philosophies and "mysticisms" are numerous, quite complex, and always expressed in languages for which English has no directly comparable terms contexts. So this humble author begs gentle forgiveness for whatever blunders he might make along these lines.

83

The first "kind," as it might erroneously be put, could be referred to as the "ascetic" type, an ASCETIC being an austere, hermit-like individual who practices strict self-denial so as to achieve "detachment" from the world of "illusions" – such detachment being thoughts of as one kind of wisdom.

That world of illusions constitutes what others think of as the phenomena of the "real" world, especially constituting all material realms, in which terrific reality-box conflicts and battles are usually waged to achieve illusionary material control and dominance within them.

The ascetic understands that the mind and consciousness can be purged of attachments and connections to the illusory realms, thereby achieving perpetual understanding and serenity with respect to the greater significant realities of the innate qualities of "pure" mind and "pure" consciousness that would not even need physical bodies to exist in.

To the ascetic, however, this can be achieved only by voluntary and strict "detachment" from all that otherwise would drag one back into the illusory and hypnotic realms of activity, physical, mental, or otherwise.

It should be emphasized that Asian ascetics in general undertake all of this detachment not specifically to "escape" anything per se, but to render Self toward attachment to, and knowing participation in, the greater and larger qualities of consciousness – which many have actually recognized as existing throughout recorded human history.

84

If all of this works, we would, in today's contemporary parlance and concepts, think of it as serenely "advanced" with respect to what is otherwise here on Earth an illusory mess, dominated by the pursuit of hypnotic gratifications that have been processed upward into ominous and awesome potentials.

Carl Sagan's fictional description of the essential nature of an "advanced civilization" reflects it as one of pure consciousness and actively possessing its greater and larger qualities.

Even our own self-destructive civilizations (that rise and fall) would hardly appreciate the arrival of a mind-messy ET civilization to save us from our own. If so, all we would want from them is to copy, or reverse-engineer, their weapons of mass destruction for purposes of our own reality boxes, from which we might not save ourselves anyway.

85

"Detachment," so as to escape life's uglier realities, more or less constitutes a second type of Eastern serenity. Even in ancient Asia, it seems that not all people desired completely to abandon participation in hypnotic illusory activities, but to achieve some kind of more elevated poise over them.

This might be thought of as "semi-detachment." Many achieved ancient sages warned against this kind of undertaking, in that such would only result in "confusions," but which anyway seems to have become very popular.

When different schools of Eastern mysticism were slowly imported (circa the early 1700s) into Europe and the Americas, this semi-detachment aspect also began its rise into popularity.

As the Western market for semi-detachment began to grow in the eighteenth century, some Eastern mystics exported themselves to the West, followed by a larger number of them in the nineteenth century. To be sure, all of these self-export individuals should be properly appreciated as "vehicles" of Eastern knowledge. But once in the West, it was discovered by them that only the "practice" of semi-detachment sold.

Several good books (noted in the bibliography) have reviewed all of this importing and exporting, some referring to it as an "invasion," others as an "epoch" involving "comparative" Western and Eastern philosophies (but which, by the way, are not really comparative).

86

There were three interconnected reasons for the Western drift toward the serenity of semi-detachment. Most Westerners could not intellectually grasp many of the most refined and important aspects of the ancient Eastern heritage, largely because there were no Western concepts or linguistic terms that the Eastern ones could precisely be translated or transliterated into.

However, within the resulting confusions (many of which were not and still aren't understood or admitted as such), most Westerners interested in Eastern mysticism also proved notoriously reluctant to abandon all, or even any, of their connections to the illusory world.

The calming serenity, and even the "ecstasies," of temporary semi-detachment were just what the Western market wanted, for thereby one could also remain at least selectively attached to the illusory realms and reality boxes one didn't want to abandon.

There was and still is nothing essentially "wrong" with this, for approaches toward "advanced" consciousness must begin somewhere, and many Eastern sages have indicated that acquisition of such is a project on-going "through many lives."

87

What might be thought of as a third type of Eastern developmental serenity is a bit more difficult to briefly review, because it does not particularly focus on achieving serenity of Self, but on collective serenity of peoples.

Even though ancient China produced two eloquent examples of this, the collective-serenity concept is today virtually alien to Westerners and even to a whole lot of Asians.

One of the chief stumbling blocks to this is that when we today think of collective peoples, we do so by depending on the modern terms of "social" or "sociology," and we have developed no other additional or more extensive frames of reference.

The term SOCIOLOGY is entirely modern, having been coined only in 1843, when, in its first rendering as a "new science," it was defined as: "The study of social ethics so as in their light to recognize truths of social development, structure, and function."

By 1873, the "social ethics' part of the original definition had been done away with, largely, it must be suspected, because a lot of important stuff goes on in the world against which any organized study of social ethics (and virtues) would be entirely inconvenient and unwanted.

The original definition was therefore junked, and replaced by a less threatening, harmless, and more ambiguous one: "The science or study of the origin, history, and constitution of human society." This definition should not be superimposed on the ancient contexts of collective serenity.

88

The venerable philosopher-sage remembered as Lao-tzu (Old Teacher) was born (c. 604 B.C.) in China during the latter part of the turbulent Chou dynasty (c. 1027-256 B.C.) that was characterized by constant warfare between the several Chinese states and by the venality and tyranny of their rulers (something of the usual story).

Lao-tzu's dates are uncertain, but it is traditionally held that he was highly educated, philosophically and intuitively wise, and was librarian at the Chou court.

As the story goes, however, at about 539 B.C., he became disgusted with the world around him, resulting in his self-imposed retirement to a monastery, eventually dying (perhaps in 515 B.C.) in an unknown place. Before he became inaccessible to the world around him, many petitioned him to write out his "wisdom" for the edification of his followers.

89

The result of his agreement to do so was the TAO-TE-KING (or CHING), that has been variously translated into English as: The Book of Reason and Virtue; The Way; The Way of Tao; The Book of the Right Way; and The Book of Tao.

The topic of TAO is obviously an extensive one incorporating many elements. The following brief review is undertaken only with respect to its serenity-enhancing aspects.

TAO is commonly translated as "the right way of life," as "Way" or "Path," and in some few cases, as "the Way of Bliss."

In its broadest sense, TAO refers to the way the universe intrinsically functions, the TAO Path being the Way-path taken by natural events. In the first instance, The Way of Tao is characterized by creativity and by regular alternations of phenomena (such as day following night, etc.) that proceed without effort.

Effortless action is illustrated, for example, by the conduct of water, which unresistingly accepts the lowest level yet wears away the hardest substance. In order to achieve effortless action, Man, following the TAO, must abjure all striving, especially that of "desire" – after which access to his innate ideal state of consciousness and being is completely attainable by transcendentalizing contemplation on the many aspects of the natural-universal Way or Path of Tao of all things and phenomena.

90

It is admittedly difficult (at least to those who think only in the contexts of "things") to concretize what TAO is, because in its first instance it isn't anything. Rather, its essence is "form-less," but out of which emerge all formative phenomena and things each in their own Way, each having thereafter their own inherent, spontaneous, and effortless developmental Path onwards.

In modern contexts, this is similar to "seeing things as they REALLY are" versus seeing them only in the contexts of what we would desire them to be – which is the same as saying seeing them not in artificial, effort-filled contexts formed only in the desire-mind. In yet other words, "what will happen will happen" when and for as long as it does, this being the manifold Way of Tao.

91

Transcendentalizing contemplation on the manifold Way of Tao at least puts one in touch with the elements and outcomes of the Paths of Tao, and starts up, so to speak, an enlarging or an advancing of consciousness with respect to "seeing" such as they ARE and WILL BE regardless of efforts of artificial mind-desire contexts set up to interfere with their Way and Paths. Seeing such will not only result in tranquility and the serenity of enlightenment, but also in spontaneous, positive, and increasing creativity and transformation that become available within the contexts of an "advanced consciousness."

It might also be thought that "seeing" such will also result in increases of intuitive insight into the nature of Paths of Tao and increase powers of prediction and the simplicity of wisdom.

Trying to change, via artificial desire, what IS only sets up resistance, and which, in the TAO, will unfold into ITS eventual outcomes.

92

In Europe, the Book of Tao was first rendered into Latin in 1788, and thereafter into other languages, including several English translations, not all of which are consistent with each other.

One basic reason for the confusions was the fact that English simply did not, and still does not, have matching concepts or terms for many of the important Chinese ones. Some translations get around this significant problem simply by not drawing attention to its existence.

However, what seems to be the best and most enlightening discussion of this problem is found in the ninth 1892 version of the Encyclopaedia Britannica under the entry for LAO-TSZE (Vol. XIV, pp. 295-298), which is also an excellent discussion of major Taoist principles.

This entry illustrates the difficulties of discussing higher and more advanced states of consciousness by reducing them into the contexts and vocabulary of lower and less advances states.

93

The venerable sage remembered by the name of Confucius (c.551-479 B.C.) was a younger contemporary of Lao-tzu, who was also born into the tremendous centuries-long wars and conflicts of the faltering Chou dynasty, of which there were some twenty-five successive ruling Dukes.

After a somewhat difficult start in life, Confucius traveled widely, was acknowledged as a learned philosopher, and was consulted by many, including rulers of various localities – but who would not put into practice his moral and ethical doctrines (here again, something of a familiar story).

He ultimately urged a system of moral ethics and statecraft aimed at preserving peace and affording people the relative serenity and stability of a just government they required.

94

Central to his concepts was the existence of JEN, for which English has not evolved a comparable and precise term. However, it seems to refer to the concept that humans are essentially born as mutually interdependent creatures all of which are innately and collectively linked by JEN – which some scholars have translated as "sympathy" coupled with "human heartedness."

But JEN is more than those two English terms alone can imply – because JEN seems to consist of an inter-shared "connectivity" among all, and thus may belong somewhere within the concepts of Jung's collective unconscious – while the "shared" part seems to fall within Velikovsky's concept of an innate "archaic telepathy," and upon which "sympathy" and "empathy" would be based.

JEN could be cooperatively "advanced" by cultivating intelligence, awareness, and insightful alertness, and also by reinforcing the virtues having to do with development of self-control, kindness, absence of offensiveness, neighborliness, fidelity, kindness, and patience.

95

Confucius insisted that the "workings" of JEN thrived and grew in energy via cooperative enhancement of human virtues, and was weakened and disoriented by discord, the threat of looming and ominous dangers, and fears that could not be resolved.

JEN is outwardly expressed in many ways, especially when people need to pull together for the common good, or for common safety, and, sometimes, for common advancement. But expressed JEN also occurs between sovereign and subjects, parent and child, elder and younger, husband and wife, and friend and friend. These expressions of JEN strongly suggest something more than mere intellectually induced behavior, something more like telepathic affinity, archaic or otherwise.

96

In its early form (before the 3rd century B.C.), Confucianism was entirely a system of ethical precepts that acknowledged the "powers" of JEN, and advocated REAL support of human virtues within the contexts of proper, correct, and cooperative conduct management of peoples – all existing within, so to speak, original and on-going JEN. Ethical certainty shared among people always inspires a kind of calmness and serenity (and perhaps something like this has reemerged into today's growing concept of "community").

The maxims of Confucius are encoded in his ANALECTS, but there is evidence that they have been tampered with and altered several times after the 3rd century B.C.

For example, during the Sung dynasty (960-1279), Neo-Confucianism introduced certain metaphysical precepts that were not incorporated into its original form (such as the concepts of heaven, the fear elements of purgatory, and hell), with the result that Confucianism began to be thought of as a religion.

The original form should more properly be thought of as a positive Way of Life and Living aimed at shared JEN serenity and positive creativity via the virtues of intuitive perception (sometimes referred to in the cultural West as "wisdom").

97

Although the "teachings" of Lao-tzu and Confucius are extensive and complex (perhaps because of latter additions to them), it seems clear enough that at least one of their mutual basic aims was to lift or advance consciousness to some level above war-consciousness, and the cruel veniality and excessive indulgences of the rulers of the time that resulted in equally excessive death and destruction of peoples.

Human virtues are always seen (even by those who have no use for them), as several clicks superior to non-virtuous inferior strata wherein conflict, discord, war, fear, and terror are psychological modes of more importance.

98

It is worthwhile pointing up that Lao-tzu and Confucius lived during the highest peak of the war epoch of the Chou dynasty, during which no less than a dozen instructional "conduct of war" books and texts have been recovered, many more having been lost.

The most continuingly famous of these war-texts was one pulled together, at approximately 530 B.C., by Sun-tzu (or by his "school"), entitled THE ART OF WAR.

Copies and translations of this book have always been continuously desired, obtained, and carefully studied throughout the whole of Asia, and shortly after translations of it were available in the West, even Napoleon I studied it in intimate detail. And what Napoleon studied so did everyone else then and since. In a new translation by Ralph D. Sawyer, this book was freshly reissued in 1994, and, one is told, vociferously devoured by, of all things, financial experts and brokers on Wall Street.

Thus, if one had to choose between THE ART OF WAR, THE BOOK OF TAO, and THE ANALECTS of Confucius, one can bet on which one would be most selected.

So, the most we can learn about "peace of mind" and achieving serenity is that we know such potentials exist, but that they are hard to constructively "sell" in any meaningful big-time way.

99

There is one interesting little tidbit regarding serenity that has become visible during the last few decades.

This has to do with SEROTONIN, now recognized as a potent cerebral synaptic inhibitor, also known as 5-hydroxytryptamine, and identical with enteramine (which is found in the enterochromaffin system of the mammalian gastrointestinal tract).

Various functions have been attributed to serotonin, but its chief interest lies in the evidence that it is, when healthy, involved as a necessary synaptic agent in the regulation of centers in the brain concerned with wakefulness, temperature regulation, blood- pressure regulation, and various other autonomic functions.

Serotonin is also recognized as a mood stabilizer and enhancer, more or less in the feel-good, calming, and serenity categories. Without these qualities or states, one tends to descend into gloom and various kinds of depression.

It is also recognized that induced worry, stress, anxiety, and fears (whether conscious, subconscious, or unconscious) can suppress its production, throwing all the regulation centers in the brain out of whack, both physiologically and mentally.

Chapter Fourteen

DO ADVANCED CIVILIZATIONS EXIST?

100

AT FIRST TAKE, it might seem odd to introduce consideration of ETs at this juncture. There is at least one important reason for doing so, briefly established as follows.

For a long time, our species has recognized the existence of the cosmos. In the cultural West, it was broadly held that not only was Mankind a created (or evolved) life form unique in the cosmos, but, having the unique greatness of intelligence, was also the top, most ideal epitome of any life, and far superior to lesser life forms.

Man was gloriously unique and alone in the universe. Furthermore, it was deemed that except for our Sun, no other stars possessed planets. So how could there be life, much less intelligence, Out There?

As we today must largely suspect, this was an illusion. But to think of it as real, the existence of intelligent life elsewhere had to be denied and rejected, along with historical evidence that intelligences from out there had occasionally visited the vicinity of Earth, and sometimes made touchdowns.

During the late 1940s, UFOs were spotted and one or more crashed in New Mexico. Whether of fact, fiction, or cover-up, two things began to happen. First, more UFOs were spotted and described; second, certain intrepid researchers began sifting historical records for evidence that "visitations" of such kind had taken place before, some of which will be mentioned ahead.

101

While squabbles went on as to whether contemporary UFOs and earlier visitations had taken place, a certain "understanding" began, and soon increased in momentum and meaningful importance.

If Others from Out There could (in the past, present, or future) manage to efficiently jump the enormities of cosmic space and distances so as to arrive in the vicinity of Earth, then they had to be viewed as "advanced."

After all, Earthlings had no idea of how to achieve any such thing, and even in today's "space-age" technology merely voyaging to the Moon, much less distant star systems, has proved to be heavy going.

102

The importance of this to the topics in this book relates to the "advanced" part, the worry and fascination of which started up distinctions between alien "advanced civilizations" and local Earth civilizations that could no longer be thought of as advanced in comparison.

However, this Earth-developed interest in advanced civilizations Out There has NOT focused on their entire nature and scope.

Instead, it has been narrowed down to focus exclusively on their "advanced technology," accompanied by two themes of hopeful interest: (1) that ETs will give it to us, or at least tell us how to achieve it; and (2) if not, then we hope we can anyway get our hands on some if it so as to "reverse engineer" it for our own at least somewhat venal and power-mongering purposes.

103

With respect to the second aspect, a tremendous literature has blossomed forth in the last fifteen years or so, which, focuses on the existence of significant cover-ups and secret governmental and scientific activity along these lines.

With all of this tremendous literature having come about, it no longer really matters if ETs exist, because the distinction between "advanced" and "not advanced" has achieved an important cultural standing in its own right that has entered the collective conscious of our entire world.

104

Prior to this development, which began in the early 1950s, all human activities, especially those scientific, that had future implications were collectively hailed as "Progress" or "progressive." Indeed, the main themes of the once called "Age of Progress" (roughly between 1884 and the advent of World War II) were so enthusiastic that it was predicted that something like a world Utopia would be achieved by the year 2000.

In this enthusiasm, the qualities of "advanced" and "not-advanced" did not have a logical or rational place, because "Progress" automatically equated to the certainty of expected and predictable advancement.

The Age of Progress (at its height during the 1920s and 1930s) was of course shattered by the horrendous debacle of World War II and the advent of the atomic bomb, the first weapon of mass destruction, and which could not be fitted into any kind of a utopian paradigm.

As a result, the once dynamic Age of Progress suddenly found itself in history's dustbins, and the word "utopia" became so intellectually "unfashionable" as to be thought of as obsolete – as did the equally embarrassing term "wisdom," the substance of which proved to have been intellectually vacated in the progressive utopia syndrome.

105

In at least a certain sense, the Age of Progress was replaced by nothing less than collective profound worries and fears as to what or which "progressive" development would ultimately lead to what or which end, i.e., to an advanced or a not-advanced end. For example, the Age of the Widening Proliferation of WMDs cannot all that much qualify as an "advanced" symptom. And neither can the Age of Vacated Wisdom.

Our present Age of UFOs commenced during the 1950s, and, to say the least of it, has risen into such high visibility that it pings on everyone's radars.

Since then, UFOs have been connected to the idea that they must originate from "advanced civilizations" elsewhere in the cosmos – if, for no other reason, than reported and radar-confirmed sightings of miles-wide "motherships" cannot yet be thought of as originating on Earth.

When the idea (or model) of such civilizations is compared to Earth civilizations altogether verging on the fearsome abyss of WMDs, etc., it is entirely possible to conclude, even if only hypothetically, that Earth's civilizations are NOT advanced, no matter if some think otherwise.

106

In any event, there remains the situation with respect to whether ETs exist Out There. Any cogitating on or contemplating of this question must incorporate two basic factors – which is to say, HONESTLY incorporate them.

One of these factors involves the enduring dimensions of the Out There, the cosmos, the universe, as they have become better and more magnificently understood as of our present times.

The first of these dimensions has to do with what is fondly referred to as the "age" of the universe, the estimation of which involves many billions upon billions of Earth's calendar years, and at least an equal amount of solar light years.

Any estimation of this time-enduring dimension extends far beyond what we would think of as great, vast, and gigantic, so much so that we do not really have conceptual frames of reference it – except, perhaps, "timeless" or "ageless" or "infinite," the latter of which implies "endlessness."

One of the second dimensions of the Out There has do with what is in it – and what IS in it can only be guesstimated as billions upon billions of galaxies, each of which are populated with billions of stars, including our own Milky Way galaxy.

The old idea that once held convincing sway was that our Sun, our local star, was the only one that had orbiting planets, and if this was the case, then there was a semblance of justification to think that Man on Earth having organic life-cum-consciousness-cum-intelligence-cum-mind/brain was unique in the ageless, infinite universe.

In the last few years, however, astronomers have discovered some several dozens of planets in the vicinity of other stars in our local galaxy alone. This implies that there are millions if not billions of planets elsewhere in the cosmos.

In turn, this implies that Earth-Man is probably Not Alone in the infinite reaches of the cosmos, the so-called "edges" of which continue to recede into even greater distances as Earthlings invent more powerful telescopes.

Considering all of this, it is no longer out of the question that organic or other kinds of life-intelligent forms could have arisen elsewhere in the Out There, some of which, billions upon billions of years ago, may even have managed to erect civilizations so advanced that Earth concepts of "advanced" may be entirely irrelevant.

The issue of intelligent life and civilizations in the Out There is no longer out of the question but is In the question – and THIS will never again depart from human awareness or suspicion unless we destroy ourselves before we might be saved from Ourselves by Others in the Out There.

107

The second of the two basic factors mentioned above has to do with whether ETs have ever made visitations to Earth.

Almost *every* culture, excepting those of the more modern West, possesses legends and myths along these lines – but which can be selectively ignored by any social system electing to do so, and so no one in those systems can be the wiser.

It would seem, however, that scholarly research of existing historical records establishing evidence of such visitations should not be ignored any more than other historical facts should be.

As most know by now, during the last thirty years a plethora of books about UFOs and ETs have appeared with respect to three general categories of the overall situation: accounts of sightings/crashes; cover-ups of UFO evidence; and, to a lesser degree, historical accounts of ET activity in ancient times.

Here, we refer specifically to the latter category, some historical accounts of which are less scholarly than others – but the whole of which clearly deserves serious attention IF historical evidence of visiting ETs exists.

108

Scholarly research has several levels of efficiency, perhaps the most pristine of which requires the researcher to discover, incorporate, and present references to documentation that is original to whatever is being researched, and which original documentation requires some kind of a working knowledge of several languages.

To this writer's knowledge, the first person to incorporate various scholarly skills with a study of ancient ET activity accounts was W. Raymond Drake. His first effort was published in England under the title SPACEMEN IN THE ANCIENT EAST (1963), and which included a list of the 289 major sources he depended on so as to begin recovering an overview of ancient ET visitations.

This writer obtained a copy of the book when it was first published, quickly wrote a letter to its author, and was rewarded with a wonderful exchange of correspondence with him that lasted for three decades.

Drake's book sold well throughout Europe and elsewhere, having been translated into several languages, but which, for some obscure reason, did not find a *very* large responsive audience in the United States. Encouraged by the European response, however, Drake thereafter went on to publish:

- Spacemen in the Ancient East (1963);
- Spacemen in the Ancient West (1974);
- Gods and Spacemen Throughout History (1975);
- Gods and Spacemen in Greece and Rome (1976);
- Gods and Spacemen in Ancient Israel (1976).

Altogether reviewed in his books is a tour de force of reports of ET visitations in ancient territories of: North America; Aztec Mexico; the Inca kingdoms of South America; India; Tibet; China; Japan; Egypt; Babylon; Israel; Greece; Rome; Scandinavia; Britain; Saxon times; Norman times; the Middle Ages; and during the Age of Reason; as well as Today.

In reviewing Drake's work, it must be remembered that the ancients almost always referred to "Spacemen" as "gods," while during the early decade of Drake's compilations, "Spacemen" was the term popularly in use, because "ETs" had not yet come into general usage.

109

Drake managed to pull together and establish that historical evidence relative to ET visitations to Earth did exist, and in a copious and available manner the extent of which had not, before him, been at all suspected.

When the double scenarios of the infinite cosmic situation regarding probable advanced ET civilizations are put together with historic evidence of their "visitations" to Earth, it becomes difficult to suppose that such civilizations don't exist.

Chapter Fifteen

"ADVANCED"?

110

IN THE CONTEXTS of this book, the foregoing review of the increasingly high probability of ET civilizations has to do with something many may not have yet realized.

That "something" is this: If only hypothetically speaking, ET civilizations are to be thought of as "advanced" (which is and has been the case since ancient times), then, by comparison, Earth civilizations are not – but instead are existing and on-going in states or conditions far less than advanced ones (exactly as some have suspected and even uttered in print).

The unavoidable implication of this is that Earth definitions (in any Earth languages) of "advanced" have begun to wobble, with the result that the term must now be followed by a question mark. For example, "advances" that have led to the wide proliferation and threat of WMDs can hardly be thought of as achieving an advanced state or condition – even if ETs should arrive to save us from them.

After all, having to live, worldwide, under the potential threat of such, maybe to be released by some unsound mind or equally unsound collective reality box, can hardly be called "advanced."

It is the case, however, that there is the hope that we (in the species collective) will somehow discover ways and means to "move beyond" the "Age of Such Ominous Threats," the general and principal solution of which is seen as advocating the restorative "peace" process in all those many places where war is.

111

Since the definitions and related concepts of "advanced" have begun to wobble, it is worthwhile reviewing the recognized definitions.

ADVANCED is, of course, an adjective that has three recognized meanings:
1. Far on in time or course;
2. Beyond the elementary or introductory;
3. Being beyond others.

The third definition is the one being applied to ET "advanced civilizations," but with an admittedly implicit meaning that does not include ours, or no longer does. Indeed, if our civilizations were "advanced," then there would be no need to use the adjective with specific reference to ET ones.

Chapter Sixteen

ON THE HYPOTHETICAL NATURE OF ADVANCED ET CONSCIOUSNESS?

112

ANY DISCUSSIONS about the nature of advanced ET consciousness must surely be hypothetical, possibly even in the extreme.

But there is one exception that departs from the hypothetical, and at least takes on borderline reality.

When advanced ET civilizations are spoken of, the "advanced" part mostly refers not to the ETs themselves, but to their advanced technology. Anyone who has taken even a minimal interest in UFOs, etc., probably has come to realize that there are large segments of interested Earth parties at rather high levels, including many notable scientists, which would like to get their hands on this advanced technology, or even fragments of it.

This for purposes of "reverse-engineering" it, presumably to be used for Earth purposes that are shrouded in deepest secrecy, but some of which can easily be imagined, such as money, competitive development, and increases of power.

What is hardly ever mentioned, however, is that advanced technology does not exist alone and of itself but must descend out of advanced minds (if "minds" is a word applicable to ETs).

This author has occasionally had the opportunity of asking a few "interested parties" about this lack of interest. Not much by way of answer was ever forthcoming. But one could get the impression that the very idea of advanced ET (read "alien" in this case) minds and/or consciousness was more awesomely threatening than their advanced technology was.

One of the Earth facts associated with this matter is that there is (with some few exceptions) great reluctance to find out what human minds and consciousness actually and more completely consist of.

As but one example of this, alien ETs might have possession of advanced forms of wisdom, the very thing on Earth that is in rather short supply, and, furthermore, is not studied and clearly not nurtured at all, much less advanced into any form of meaningful efficiency.

113

So, for starters, if advanced ET civilizations do exist, we must admit that we have no way of knowing how long they have existed. However, considering the seemingly infinite dimensions of the universe, such could have gotten underway billions and billions of years ago, perhaps long before even our local Sun or galaxy came into existence.

Although this possibility boggles a little, there is one thing about it that might be thought of as relatively correct: that such advanced civilizations did not happen only "yesterday" in cosmic time, or even during the four billion years attributed to Earth's own existence.

Hypothetically speaking, it is entirely possible that ET civilizations may have had billions of years to have advanced themselves, and so, in all likelihood, such advancement would have achieved many directions in addition to their technological ones. If this were to be the case, then we have no real way of comprehending what the advanced civilizations themselves might consider as advanced.

One factor about all this seems clear enough, even if only hypothetically so. Such ET civilizations could not possibly sit around through billions of years and not come to realize that what we now call mind-consciousness could be advanced from one state, to another, and yet another, and so forth, up to and including ET advanced wisdom.

If not, then we would have to think that ET civilizations consist of nothing more than great billions-of-years-long clunks of committed materialists, interested only in upgrading various kinds of "hardware" into this or that advanced status.

This would be ideal and most understood by interested Earth parties, because, as it happens, this is the major, most dynamic, and most recognizable model of Mankind, which, as the species homo sapiens sapiens, appeared on Earth only some 35,000 to 50,000 years ago. (Our present species appellation, by the way, is Latin for "Man who is intelligent, and knows that he is," this being cast as a hopeful appellation that might be somewhat premature.)

114

If one wants to hypothesize on what of their mind-consciousness that advanced ET civilizations might have advanced through billions of years, we, unfortunately, have only the lenses of our own basic Earth model to speculate through.

Even so, there is one possibility that can be considered, one which certain exobiologists (who study alien life forms) sometimes theorize about.

There is the possibility that all organic life forms in the universe have certain innate things in common, such as relatively similar biological processes. If so, then all biologically intelligent life forms might also have certain basic similarities – such as, for example, innate intelligence or something that equates to it. It is quite well known on Earth that intelligence can be advanced, although few great efforts are broadly undertaken to do so.

115

Biologically intelligent life forms throughout the cosmos might also be innately in possession of "archaic telepathy," which might be tolerably advanced beyond its archaic state if their intelligence has become sufficiently advanced enough to realize the usefulness of doing so.

This would alleviate the dependency of advanced civilizations on electromagnetic forms of information transfer via technological instruments, and even we today would think of this as advanced – although not many on Earth want this to happen.

Here on Earth, human contactees and abductees of ETs

report almost unanimously that ETs communicate via telepathy and can even "read" the minds of Earthlings by the same method.

From the ET viewpoint, this mode of communicating would certainly save them from having to learn our 30,000 Earth languages and dialects. They also wouldn't have to lug around physical computer language translating equipment in their otherwise technologically advanced spacecraft.

While telepathy here on Earth is excluded from positive development and enhancement, its actual existence is at least tacitly accepted everywhere, even by those who object to it.

If one examines all that has been observed during our present Age of UFOs, it turns out that the telepathic connection seems, on the surface, to be about the only thing we have in common with ETs. But this is a life-mind-consciousness connection rather than one having any form of physicality.

In any event, life-mind-consciousness telepathy must basically be similar everywhere. Our form of it, however, mostly exists in its innate archaic state, whereas the telepathy of ETs appears to have been advanced beyond that.

One implication not only of this similar telepathic aspect, but also including all other observed and reported ET evidence, is that ETs have recognized the "bigness" of life-mind-consciousness and have advanced the use of theirs into realms we cannot comprehend.

The basic reason behind why we cannot is that we have not yet recognized the "bigness" of our own life-mind-consciousness. If we consider the potentials of our own "bigness," we might, in many aspects, be more similar to ETs than we have hereto thought.

116

If ET mind-consciousness-intelligence has advanced beyond the allure of gross materialism, they might have, already billions of years ago, realized that matter is not really and only physical matter, but encapsulated energy patterns that can be disassociated at one point and reassembled by "beaming" it elsewhere.

Advanced civilizations might have advanced enough to

realize that innate consciousness itself (which is probably the basis of innate intelligence), is not "nothing," but something altogether composed of manifold potentials that can be advanced from their potential state into – well, who knows what.

Coming toward the end of this hypothesizing, there is no real reason to suppose that life-intelligence-consciousness absolutely requires a biological body to house it. This is simply a matter of what comes first - a biological body or a life-intelligence-consciousness. On Earth, this kind of thing so far represents an optional reality-box "take-your-pick" affair.

117

Finally, it must be wondered if advanced ET civilizations have somehow managed to surmount the fear-terror-war thing that remains endemic on Earth.

Here, for once, the Earth model of human mind-consciousness comes in handy – because it has been recognized that fear, terror, and war are NOT concrete things-in-themselves, but essentially consist of little more than certain lesser psychological states of mind-consciousness, the dynamisms of which can be induced or reduced.

If the whole of our collective mind-consciousness were not "bigger" than such certain lesser psychological states, then our species might have terminally self-destructed long ago.

And, speculating once again, so would have civilizations Out There that might not have advanced toward this particular realization and permanently acquired and advanced its full implications.

It is certainly clear enough that anything that is extremely focused on fear, terror, and war cannot last too long even on Earth, and certainly not even in the smallest, most tiny micro fraction of a billion years.

118

The one important thing about all of this is that Earth people everywhere, and through time, have recognized that human mind-consciousness does have many more innate categories of psychological states than those representative of fear, terror, and war. This recognition itself can be thought of as "advanced" over non-recognition of it.

Life-intelligent-mind-consciousness might, all in all, have a billion psychological states at its disposal. This estimate might be a slight exaggeration, but if such did not have very many categories of psychological states in addition to those of war, fear, and terror, well then, zippo and down the drain long ago.

Fear, terror, and war exact awful and terrible tributes on their behalf, but when their "work" is said and done, it is other of our more positive psychological categories that commence reconstruction of things.

This kind of thing, by the way, is the archetype in the collective unconscious everywhere understood and pictured as the Phoenix Rising From The Ashes.

PART FOUR

WISDOM? EARTH VERSIONS OF IT, ANYWAY

Chapter Seventeen

SOME HISTORICAL ASPECTS OF WISDOM

119

ANYONE WANTING to find information about wisdom doesn't have to get too far along in the search in order to discover that information about it soon peters out.

There are probably a number of important reasons. But one of them clearly has to do with the fact that wisdom is closely connected to peace, while peace, in turn, is generally thought to become established by the "workings" of wisdom.

Now, mankind, humanity, our species, or whatever, have what is called "history."

But in a bigger overview of that history, it most extensively consists of the recounting of wars, of various types of conquering, of military successes or failures, of political and other similar kinds of disruptions, and of the rise and fall not only of "leaders," but also of whole societies and civilizations themselves.

120

Periods of peace are mentioned only marginally. The result of this is that there is no history of peace itself, because historians jump from one period of opportunistic war, terror, and fear to another and another, ad infinitum.

Therefore, peace, and its actual history, does not anywhere loom all that large in historical consciousness.

Even when peace is briefly referred to, there is NO mention of any kind of role that wisdom might have played in achieving it.

So, there is virtually no history of wisdom.

121

In instances where wisdom IS discussed, one finds, even in ancient times, that it has been consigned over to that department referred to as "philosophy," which is rarely associated with practical matters.

Even in our more recent times, the modern departments of "psychology" and "sociology" have not yet advanced enough to incorporate wisdom into any important official consideration whatsoever.

However, one can find that wisdom figures as "something" in various kinds of contemplative social groupings, but whose main characteristic is their desired and sustained "detachment" from the rest of the world near and far.

122

The etymology of the English word WISDOM seems not to have been clearly established. The WIS part is associated with Old English terms such as WISSIAN, meaning to show the way, give information about. At about 888 and 1000 A.D., these meanings had apparently incorporated into WISSDOM or WISDOME that seemed to signify "soundness of judgment in the choice of means and ends; and, capacity of judging rightly in matters relating to life and conduct."

For some time thereafter, though, the term seems to have been used principally in the contexts of "divine metaphysics," in whose supreme realms wisdom was a complete and unsullied full part, and from which it could, if and when it did, "dribble" down into the hearts and minds of those had become sufficiently insightful enough to take notice of it.

No disrespect is intended in the above, because the category of divine metaphysics implies an innate sense of "the beyond," and which has surfaced everywhere and in all cultures of the world – which clearly means that it is a category inherent in the consciousness of our species, and in the collective unconscious as well therein having several archetype images of its own.

123

By about 1360, what can only be thought of, in today's terms, as a paradigm jump seems to have taken place via new definitions, to wit: "A piece of wisdom; a wise thing to do; a wise action or proceeding." These definitions obviously apply more significantly to secular human activities taking place more or less separated from of the divine metaphysical category.

Since those early times, the categories of divine and secular wisdom have come down almost independently of each other, the secular category having been increasingly assigned over to "philosophy."

124

There is, however, a small problem with the term WISE. Between about 950 and about 1572, it seems to have principally been used to signify "Manner, mode, habit, style, fashion, in fashion, following after the fashion."

Collectively taken, these terms have referred to what we call "trendy" or following styles that are up-to-date, smart, and au courant, inclusive of fashionable and trendy thinking.

Behind these earliest principle definitions, there was emerging a sort of secondary one that had more fully risen to the surface by about 1508, to wit: "Having or exercising sound judgment or discernment; characterized by good sense and prudence; capable of judging what is right or fitting, and being disposed to act accordingly; having the ability to perceive and adopt the best means to achieve an end." (This last definition will significantly figure in the pages ahead.)

At first take, it would seem that these definitions, taken altogether, are, in their scope, what is properly meant by "wise" and by "wisdom."

But it can be shown that they are ambiguous in the extreme for one simple reason: the concept of "virtue" is omitted from them, with the result that they can be used in support of virtue-less means to achieve virtue-less ends within which "wise" and "wisdom" are absent.

125

Our English terms "wise" and "wisdom" have been derived from very early Germanic cultures of the Nordic type, in which wisdom was probably a concept affiliated with shamans and seers of one kind or another. So exact equivalents to them are not really going to be found in the rest of the world.

Instead, the nearest equivalent is found very widespread in the concept generally expressed as "conduct of life for its betterment."

There is evidence that this concept existed even in pre-historic cultures. All ancient civilizations times accumulated such life-conduct literature, basically through sayings and proverbs handed down to generations as the crystallized results of experience, and which, if proven workable enough, could be referred to as "wisdom," on the understanding that unless it proved workable for the betterment of life it was not.

Now, it should be pointed up that what wisdom actually can or should consist of often becomes ambiguous, and also that the concept of "conduct of life for its betterment" seems to slip away quite easily. Please bear this in mind.

126

Perhaps the best known of ancient collections of such life-conduct proverbs is that of the Egyptian Ptah-hotep, dating from about 2500 B.C. This collection is referred to as "The Egyptian Book of Wisdom."

But here it really should be understood that "Wisdom" is principally an English term, and that the English language did not begin to coalesce until approximately 800 A.D., i.e., about 3,000 years after 2500 B.C.

The next best-known collections are found in China, in the writings of Lao-tzu and Confucius, produced in the sixth century B.C., followed by those of Mencius in the fourth century B.C.

In India, the "eight-fold Path" of Buddha (c.563-483 B.C.) is clearly concerned with conduct of life for its betterment.

127

Of far greater influence in the West has been the literature of the Hebrew people, with more specific reference to the philosophical parts of the Old Testament and the Apocrypha. Perhaps the most important of these to the conduct of life are the books of Job, Proverbs, and Psalms, and the apocryphal book called The Wisdom of Solomon.

Also of great influence in the West was the "wisdom" literature of the early Greeks that long preceded the appearance of their great philosophers. The writings of Hesiod (eighth century B.C.), and Theognis (sixth century B.C.), summed up, in poetic form, the maxims of their traditional ethics and morality.

128

However, the first full statement of the embodiment of the classic Greek concept of conduct-of-life wisdom came with Socrates (c.470-399 B.C.), who insisted that virtue and knowledge were one, and that if men failed to live well, it was because of ignorance of what virtue really was. He had no doubt that if men knew what virtue was, they would embody it in their conduct.

The stress on wisdom based on virtue was continued by his disciple, Plato, but who conceptualized three departments of human nature: the appetites; emotions distinctly human; and reason. Of these, reason was the most important, for only as impulse and feeling were governed by reason could conduct be saved from excess and chaos.

These early Greek beginnings of wisdom that focused on virtue were soon lost to the world. In 366 B.C., the most famous pupil of Socrates, Alexander III (356-323 B.C.) of Macedonia succeeded to Macedonia's throne in 336 B.C., and soon set about by "quieting the restive cities of Greece" so as to "unite" them under the control of Macedonia.

The young Alexander then went on to "take" the rest of Asia Minor, including the Persian Empire and Babylon. He attempted to "take," but somewhat failed to do so, the area now known as Afghanistan, and then North India where hardships forced him back to his united Greece.

Undaunted, he "took" Egypt and several smaller countries now having disappeared from view - after which he was referred to as Alexander the Great. As admittedly fascinating and romantic as his life was, the body count left behind was quite vast, and does not seem the product of too much virtuousness.

In Alexander's effort to establish and spread Pan-Hellenic ideals, many texts of the Greek philosophers were destroyed or lost, only to start being recovered during the great European Renaissance dated from the fifteenth to the seventeenth centuries.

129

Some date the beginning of the Modern Age to the Renaissance (meaning "Rebirth," and/or the Rebirth of Knowledge).

As something of a shortened timeline, the Renaissance was followed by the Age of Reason, then by the Age of Technology, and then by the Age of Progress that was abruptly abandoned as of World War II.

The Age of Progress was replaced, by the Age of Weapons of Mass Destruction that was made possible when the otherwise profitable Age of Technology began to be emphasized in the early 1800s. The Age of WMDs is the result of late modern technological developments thought by many to be "advanced."

130

In its modern contexts, the topic of wisdom has aroused only sparse interest and study, and then only in philosophical theorizing undertaken by diverse philosophical thinkers. But even if sparse, the theorizing has caused many to wonder if there are any characteristic traits that wisdom-like thinking might share in common.

In the more modern contexts of philosophy, there is agreement that two shared traits stand out, which are referred to as "Reflectiveness" and "Judgment."

By "Reflectiveness" is meant "the habit of considering events, beliefs, and ideas in the light of their grounds and consequences." Study of this Reflectiveness usually ends up in observations indicating that it is of a peculiar intuitive kind, in the sense that it is not arrived at by argument, or easily defended by it – such "argument" otherwise being the principal method by which reason and rationality are established as such.

"Judgment" refers to the concept that "there is a wisdom of ends as well as of means pursued in order to obtain them."

It seems that the Judgment aspect has undergone the most scrutiny, especially with respect to the ever-on-going conflict between the "good" and the "bad." During the twentieth century, several philosophers concluded that settlement of this conflict "is beyond reason," on the grounds that judgments of good and bad are not at all expressions of knowledge, but only of desires and emotion.

For these philosophers, there is properly no such thing as wisdom regarding knowledge of the intrinsic good because knowledge is more commonly confined to means to obtain ends whose consequences are questionable and unknowable in advance.

131

The bottom philosophical line of all this refers to the debatable question as to whether individual wisdom is, on the average, increasing. But even if not, it is generally held, if somewhat optimistically, that the opportunity for it is.

132

In any event, the existence of the wisdom category is, like that of archaic telepathy, very old, for in the collective unconscious there are contained no less than three recognizable archetypes for it.

One of these most frequently portrayed consists of an "old" bearded man suggesting long experience, and whose eyes, variously portrayed, are large and limpid suggestive of depth of knowledge, and which are sometimes glowing which is suggestive of enlightenment.

Another one of these archetypes, once popular especially in the middle "dark" Ages, pictures a youth holding a lantern, advancing and illuminating the way so as to dispel some overly dark background scenario.

There is also the "Sophia" archetype, usually clearly identified as the primordial anima-feminine wisdom-woman, but who goes by many other assigned names in different cultures. If she abandons him, Man cannot be saved until he finds her again.

The Sophia archetype is closely related to the early Greek myth of Athene, who was born from out of the head or mind of Zeus and thus represents wisdom-thought and wisdom-thinking that radiates outward. Thus, if wisdom-thinking ceases to radiate outward, then Man must live in a wisdomless world until he can start it up again.

Chapter Eighteen

VIRTUE – AND ITS OPPOSITES

133

IT SEEMS ADVISABLE to commence this section by discussing the opposites to virtue, because the nature and identities of the opposites are vastly more familiar, bigger in effect, and of very larger "reality" than those of virtue.

Indeed, within the contexts of this book, one of the opposites of virtue is the extreme proliferation during our present times of WMDs, which opposition could turn out to be the biggest of all time, second only to a meteor impact large enough to terminate all but single cell life forms, and perhaps a fair share of those, too.

134

The opposites of virtue have been present for a very long time, apparently dating back into our species nebulous antediluvian pre-history. They were clearly and broadly proliferating in the times of Lao-tzu and Confucius.

Indeed, in his excellent translation of THE ANALECTS OF CONFUCIUS (originally published in 1938), Arthur Waley pointed up that Confucius complained that "the Way of Goodness [had been] long ago discarded by the rulers of the world in favor of the Way of violence and aggression."

With one significant exception, however, it is not necessary to undertake an extensive historic exposition of what happened along these lines, all of it being rather same-old same-old through the many centuries down until today.

135

The exception involves a book by Nicolo Machiavelli (1469-1527) posthumously printed in 1532, entitled THE PRINCE, which describes the means by which a prince may gain and maintain his power.

In the book, Machiavelli expounded his "political theory" which consisted of the view that politics is amoral and that any means however unscrupulous can justifiably be used in achieving political power – including expedient devices characterized by cunning, duplicity, naughty cleverness, or bad faith.

Excepting for the perpetually naive, something along these lines had of course been understood all along, but had never, it seems, been codified into an objectively instructional edifice – although Sun-tzu's ART OF WAR (mentioned earlier) seems to have been something of an ancient predecessor.

It is quite understandable that political structures had always tried to hide or conceal from public view their amoral workings. But with the publication of THE PRINCE, here they were for all to read and hear about – alongside the idea that since politics was amoral in the first place, seizing upon unscrupulous means were "justifiable" in the second place.

This seems to be just what those of unscrupulous leanings wanted to hear – that their unscrupulous workings were justified in order to surmount unscrupulous workings of others, i.e., same-old same-old in sort of a closed loop fashion.

There is no way of knowing the total sales volume of this book, but it has widely and in most languages been in print ever since, and even during the twentieth century was much in demand and often was required reading in universities of supposedly "higher" educations.

It turned out that Machiavellianism (as it became known) was utterly translatable into fields other than politics – into, for example, the fields of business, finance, economy, strategy planning, sociology management, the sciences, war games, media, concealment of UFOs, development of WMDs, and even into the realms of the arts, including culture mongering.

Thus, in a certain but specific sense, Machiavellianism became justifiably institutionalized so as to be able to deal with means that are not really justifiable in any bigger picture of human survival per se.

Needless to say, elements of virtue-wisdom would at least be inconvenient within the on-going working realms of Machiavellianism, and which have no real need of such in the first place.

136

While the opposites of virtue are easy enough to identify, and even actually experience in painful reality, there are several conceptual problems with respect to establishing what virtue is.

Concepts of virtue are usually arrived at by comparing them to whatever is thought of as VICE, which is defined as "Moral depravity or corruption."

However, it is quite well understood that different societies have different concepts of what is moral or amoral, and so such societies establish different realities about what vice can be thought to consist of or not. So a great deal of ambiguity can enter in wherever virtue is defined by comparing it to vice.

Since there are so many of them, versions of vice-amorality seem more like smaller pictures in the larger picture of human nature as a whole.

In the light of this, efforts of certain social systems to impose their moral values on other social systems represent little more than conflicts among smaller pictures. Even when such activities are successful, they can be little more than temporary – for different concepts of morality will arise again and again.

This situation has been studied by many noted philosophers – with the on-going result that hardly anything about it has been resolved across the boards.

137

Another familiar method or construct with respect to determining what virtue might be consists of assuming that virtue represents the "good" while its opposites represent the "bad." But this again introduces ambiguity, and in any event is always relative to different societies that have different considerations about good and bad.

138

It is assumed that wisdom is intimately linked to "the good," which, in turn, is thought to be the same as virtue.

In attempting to track down information about virtue, it can be discovered, rather surprisingly, that the otherwise exhaustive Encyclopedia of Philosophy (referred to earlier) does not have a main entry for it.

However, the Encyclopedia's index lists thirty-seven references to it and mentions, along the way, several noted philosophers, with the last reference indicating "See also, GOOD, RIGHT."

139

The Encyclopedia's longish main entry for GOOD, THE, begins as follows: "Following Aristotle, most philosophers have distinguished between intrinsic good and non-intrinsic good. An intrinsic good is something valuable of and in itself; a non-intrinsic good is something valuable by virtue of its relationship to an intrinsic good."

Thus commences a rather involved conceptual snarl that has not become entirely straightened out by the end of the entry.

In English, INTRINSIC is defined as: "Belonging to the essential nature or constitution of a thing; originating or situated within the body or part being acted on." The English term is derived from the Latin INTRINSECUS meaning "inward, inwardly," closely linked to the Latin INTRA, also meaning within.

On their surface, these definitions seem straightforward enough, and so wisdom, the good, and virtue, can be thought of as "things" in themselves AS their intrinsic selves having their own intrinsic real realities. There is no argument here, since such may actually be the case.

However, as has been discussed, it seems that wisdom, the good, and virtue must, in any practical terms, be determined as existing via comparisons to or judgment of something else – such as the intrinsic nature of the bad, the ugly, the unscrupulous, etc., the latter of which are always intrinsically embarked on collision courses with intrinsic wisdom, the good, and virtue.

This is something that Lao-tzu might have understood, and

probably did, in that all things in the Way of Tao unfold within the contexts of their own intrinsic nature, the unfoldment of each "thing" having their own intrinsic outcomes or results that, in the end, are either positive or negative.

140

In the cultural West, the bad, the ugly, the unscrupulous, etc., have been judged, through and through, as having no intrinsic VALUE, and which indeed is the case in the negative sense.

But even so, such do have intrinsic MEANING as well as IMPLICATIONS in that their unfoldments trend toward various kinds of destruction whether small or enormous.

Because the bad, the ugly, and the unscrupulous have traditionally been THOUGHT to have no intrinsic value, philosophical examination of their "place" in philosophical overviews of life and existence has been rather sparse, whereas much philosophical study has been focused of what is thought to have intrinsic value.

141

One of the points of the immediately foregoing discussion has to do with wisdom-making, and those who make it who can be called Wisdomers.

That point is this. Unless wisdomers can recognize the intrinsic meanings and implications of the unfoldment of the bad, the ugly, etc., as well as the potentializing outcomes and results of such, then their wisdom workings will clearly be inefficient – at least as long as the bad, the ugly, and so forth are lurking around.

It would be obvious that including such recognitions into the Art of Wisdom is actually necessary – if wisdom is to be called wisdom.

142

So, it is worthwhile examining the definitions of VIRTUE. In English (and in the sexist sense typical of the eighteenth century and earlier), this term is defined as:

1) Conformity to a standard of right:
2) A particular moral excellence (ambiguous as we have seen);
3) A commendable quality or trait;
4) Manly strength, courage, valor, merit;
5) A capacity to act with potency;
6) Chastity, especially in a woman.

If one can get past the sexist implications of these definitions (which, by the way, have existed for quite a long time), it can be observed that all of them refer, in one way or another, to CHARACTER defined as:

- The complex of mental and ethical traits marking an individual, group, or nation;
- One of the attributes or features that make up and distinguish the individual;
- A feature used to separate distinguishable things into categories.

143

The term VIRTUE is taken into English from Latin from VIRTUT-VIRTUS, a combined concept first consisting of "living strength" of character, and second (for additional emphasis) of "manliness" and "virility."

Today, this combined definition can seem entirely sexist, and be thought of as referring principally to extremely macho types. But in its early Latin contexts, the definitions fall into the mystical category having to do with virility of life itself.

At any rate, "virtut-virtus" seems more to have been assigned to Roman gods and goddesses who were somehow in charge of life and its workings, although such could also be attributed to male individuals who demonstrated living strength of character, and such were usually considered "favored" by the deities.

However, these traits, including the masculine connotations, were also assigned to females demonstrating living strength of character, and who, in their roles as priestesses, seers, and sibyls, were greatly paid attention to in their intuitive contact with the wisdom category, just as such were in Egypt, Greece, and Babylonia.

The early origins of our term "virtue" thus applied to a kind of upstanding, pro-creative strength of character, the intrinsic value and meaning of which our present generations seem to have lost touch with.

The Latin VIRTUS closely corresponds to the Chinese TE, which refers to the specific quality of "virtue" latent in everything. It is important to point up that neither the Chinese TE nor the Latin VIRTUS conceptualized virtue as opposed to vice. TE and VIRTUS referred to, as it were, an innate energy that was generative.

As described by Arthur Waley in the Introduction to his "Analects of Confucius," TE, "In individuals is a force or power closely akin to what we call character, and frequently contrasted with LI, 'physical force'."

There are some confusions with respect to "character" that can be resolved by considering one of its seldom used definitions, i.e., "the complex of mental and ETHICAL (emphasis added) traits marking an individual, group, or nation."

This TE or VIRTUS character is admittedly difficult to recognize amid ongoing rivers of "vice." It basically seeks to establish, as the old saying goes, that Man is innately basically good, but gets wrecked by life's corruptions and moral depravities.

144

In its major entry for THE GOOD, the Encyclopedia of Philosophy broaches a discussion about "The Highest Good."

The concept of the highest good has been most notably present among early philosophers, such as Aristotle and Thomas Aquinas, who held that human beings share a common nature or essence.

For Aristotle, man was essentially or by nature a rational "animal," rationality being the one significant trait distinguishing him from the "beasts." Consequently, man's highest good will consist in the exercise of his rational powers, or at least in contemplation of them. According to Aquinas, this "tendency" may "lie dormant or be perverted," but "it cannot be eradicated."

Well, although "rational powers" obviously constitute a category somewhere in the totality of innate human consciousness, and this category sometimes unfolds its intrinsic nature, it is to be wondered where man's vastly more familiar episodes and epics of irrationality come from.

It is at least somewhat clear that our present Age of WMDs cannot lay claim to too much rationality. It is also clear that if the Age of WMDs intrinsically unfolds itself to its intrinsic End, that end might eradicate what Aquinas referred to as a "tendency that cannot be eradicated."

However, it must be pointed up that the wisdom of Aristotle and Aquinas could not have incorporated even the very idea of the intrinsic nature of WMDs. In fact, hardly anyone could have – until the Age of WMDs was upon us.

145

Briefly returning now to the English definitions of VIRTUE, there is one that refers to "an angel of the fifth highest rank."

Something now depends on what one thinks "an ANGEL" is, but two definitions are given as "A spiritual being superior to man in power and intelligence; and, a messenger or HARBINGER," the latter term referring to "one who pioneers or initiates a major change; also, precursor, presage, or forerunner."

Before one topples over laughing, it needs to be said that numerous "angel" archetypes exist within the immense scope of the collective unconscious, and that conscious expressions of them turn up all of the time.

Although whether angels might be beings in their intrinsic right, connections to the idea of them in the collective unconscious can only mean one thing – that in the collective unconscious there are kinds of psychological pattern "matches" for them.

The definition of the angel of virtue establishes that it is one of "the fifth highest rank." This arithmetically implies that there are four lower or lesser ranks beneath. This could mean that there are, in the whole of human consciousness, categories that rank beneath or above each other. This also could imply that lower ranking categories containing opposites to virtue might rank somewhere in the vicinity of minus zero.

One cannot insist that this is the case, but it is rather amusing to contemplate.

In any event, in angelical lore of long tradition, the angel of wisdom is referred to as Pistis Sophia, "pistis" referring, in Latin, to an intrinsic, ovulating, growing seed.

Chapter Nineteen

COMPLAINTS, GRUMBLINGS, AND LAMENTS ABOUT MANKIND

146

THE FOLLOWING discussions about Mankind are principally focused only within the contexts of the familiar Modern Age, the exact beginning of which is hard to nail down.

Some hold that the beginning ascended out of the European Renaissance that began in earnest in about 1500, which incorporated the idea of the rebirth of knowledge, which, during the preceding Dark Ages, had been limited to within the confines of various ideologies.

Others assert that the beginning occurred only during the post-Renaissance decades of the 1600s, the latter decades of which inspired the Age of Reason that flowered during the 1700s.

At about the mid-1800s, however, there arose the idea and conviction that all earlier forms of knowledge should be retired because scientific knowledge was superior to all other forms, and that increasing accumulation of scientific knowledge would ultimately replace all other kinds of it – with the proviso of "the sooner, the better."

When the Modern Age is remembered today, its chief characteristics are recognized as not only consisting of modern scientific knowledge per se, but also of modern prospects of theoretical and technological scientific advancement serenely untroubled by having no need to examine earlier forms of knowledge considered obsolete.

147

The promised potentials of scientific advancement almost immediately inspired the notion of an Age of Progress during which it was earnestly and convincingly predicted that Utopia on Earth would be achieved by the year 2000.

The Age of Progress, with its hypnotic, alluring, and charismatic features, was still underway when this author was born in the early 1930s, and he remembers its exciting literature and posters proclaiming, among other encouraging positive outlooks, that "We Are Participating in the Age of Progress." This author admits youthfully sharing in the optimistic predictions, in that he had the possibility of living until 2000 and thus would be able to enjoy the forthcoming Utopia.

The advent of World War I, and the Great Depression, did not at all put dents into the thrilling prospects of the Age of Progress, and neither did the ominous foreshadows and actuality of World War II.

But the advent of the Atomic Bomb and its implications did, and so the Age of Progress, with its utopian expectations, was quietly retired, and many today do not realize that it once existed.

148

Through all of this something occurred that has hardly ever been recognized. As the Ages of Reason, Science, and Progress ascended, interest in wisdom plummeted in direct proportion.

After all, reason, science, and progress had, inwardly within them, their own intrinsic "wisdom," which would unfold not only in meaning, but also in VALUE, as such were increasingly developed and perfected.

149

The advent of the Post-Modern Age can easily be dated back to the early 1960s, if not a few years earlier. But it might be a little difficult to recognize this, if it is not understood that the basic concepts of the Modern Age were intimately affiliated with the Age of Science in which it was conceptualized that anything that could not be "made scientific" was irrelevant and of no possible modern interest.

The essence of the otherwise almost inscrutable advent of post-Modernism was, perhaps, somewhat formalized by the publication of a small yet potent book entitled SCIENCE IS NOT ENOUGH (1967) written by Vannevar Bush (1890-1974). The title of this book "says it all," and so its contents need not be covered here. But WHO Vannevar Bush was does need to be reviewed.

For starters, he is credited with designing the differential analyzer, one of the earliest computers. During World War II, he administered the U.S. war effort to utilize and improve military technology. He directed such programs as the development of the first atomic bomb, the perfection of radar, and the mass production of sulfa and penicillin. He was a vice president of M.I.T., and a president of the Carnegie Institution of Washington. He worked closely with five Presidents of the United States.

If THIS obviously important scientist/physicist, himself having aided in the production of the first atomic bomb, says "Science is not enough," one should be able "to take it to the bank."

However, post-modern contexts should not be thought of as being anti-science per se, such referring to the concept that "science is not enough."

The explicit and implicit meaning of Vannevar Bush's SCIENCE IS NOT ENOUGH is that other contexts exist that should begin to undergo examination for THEIR intrinsic meaning and value to the future.

150

But there are certain obscure difficulties that, as they stand unexamined, do not exactly facilitate such excursions into the intrinsic meanings and values of other things.

As but one example, there is the issue of MANKIND and what it consists of. We all now conceptualize mankind as the on-going collective populations of all peoples not only in the present, but also in the departing past and oncoming future.

We cannot be sure that peoples in the ancient past considered it this way or under a similar word, but in English the term was present as of about 1300 when, although its origins are said to be "obscure," it referred to "human beings in general" as well as to "the nature of man," and to "human nature."

With the exception, in modern scientific times, of the denial that human nature existed, the early definitions seem to have come down to us relatively intact.

151

What has not come down to us intact are ways in which mankind has been viewed. In its original sense, and in examples of how it was used, it was applied as an honorific conveying nobility, homage, reverence, and esteem, particularly in some collectively superior sense.

This honorific profile of mankind seems to have held until about 1510, when it apparently began to be noticed that mankind contained certain "diseases," which we today would think of as mental or psychological. The realization apparently caused quite a stir at the time, which aroused much commentary.

In 1611, the stir inspired someone named Shaks to comment that if the extent of such "diseases" were fully known, it would cause "one tenth of mankind to hang themselves."

Thereafter, it appears that contemplation of and fascination with the "diseases" increased exponentially to a point where the "diseases" loomed very large, eventually eclipsing the noble and esteemed parts of mankind.

Something of this can be seen to be the case for at least the last two hundred years, during which whenever awful things make their appearance, the ultimate blame tends to be placed squarely and collectively on Mankind and how terrible it is – which is to say, how awful we all are – sometimes expressed via the slang idiom of "Mankind sucks."

Well, now, it is quite clear (or at least it should be) that not all individuals incorporated within Mankind are fixated on and devote themselves to works that manifest and concretize the awful. Only certain "segments" within it proceed along these lines, and many suspect, if not realize, that such segments more actually constitute a rather dismal minority.

152

In conceptualizing Mankind as the total collective of all humans, one cannot, in the end, really escape the fact that the collective not only has physical bodies, but also collective minds and collective consciousness.

The collective bodies can be perceived as being and remaining separate. But collective minds and consciousness exchange and share information and "realities," and which sharing is one of their most principal functions and "duties."

In this context, the collective translates into what we know to be "mass" consciousness, which perforce has to include all forms of it, including the sub-conscious, the unconscious, and the meta-consciousness.

It is also understood that the contexts of mass consciousness can fluctuate and shift around according to what kinds of information and meanings are being incorporated into, or disincorporated from, it.

A compelling example of this is evidenced by tracing the shift of mass consciousness meanings and definitions of Mankind downward from the superlative toward perceptions of mankind as awful.

Therefore, it is not absolutely necessary to think that "one tenth of Mankind needs to hang themselves" simply because of a mere fluctuation of collective consciousness about it, which is anyway happening all of the time.

In any event, wisdom, if there is to be any, cannot be completely governed by such shifting and fluctuating.

153

Something along these lines can be said, if not exactly so, about our OTHER important collective appellation, HUMANITY, used in English at about 1380 when it first referred to: "The quality or disposition of being human; behavior or disposition towards others as befits a man. Civility, courtesy, politeness, good behavior, kindness as shown in courteous or friendly acts;

obligingness; disposition to treat human beings and animals with consideration and compassion; kindness; benevolence."

These definitions of course refer to individuals who are disposed to demonstrate them as something of value and meaning, and in demonstrating them it could be said that one has humanity. They also, by the way, echo the concerns of Confucius and others who have appeared here and there.

By about 1430 the term was translated upwards beyond the lesser scope of individuals when it was collectivized to mean: "The quality or condition of being human; human-hood; human faculties or attributes collectively; human nature; man in the abstract."

This latter definition is at some distance from the original definitions, for it is rather difficult to consider, for example, politeness or benevolence in the "abstract," excepting in philosophical discourse.

154

During the early 1800s, the term HUMANITARIAN entered the picture, the definitions of which held that "man's duty is chiefly or wholly comprised in the advancement of the welfare of the human race; having regard for the interests of humanity or mankind at large."

With no disrespect intended toward the greatly appreciated value of humanitarians who, because of the awful minority, are overworked everywhere in the world, our present concept of "humanitarianism" more or less has come to focus not on the "welfare of the [whole] human race" per se, but mostly on ameliorating the cruel hardships of those many who have become ignominious victims of various kinds of destruction.

155

Thus, although Science has achieved very many deserved credits, it has not proven to be not enough to restore or reaffirm the lost noble status of our most superlative appellations as Mankind and Humanity.

So, like Vannevar Bush and many others, one must begin to wonder where-o-where our other resources are. Wherever they might be, they clearly do not exist in the lower, or lowest, ranks of human consciousness out of which there have arisen the products, and fears of them, of WMD Armageddon.

PART FIVE

WISDOMERS?

Chapter Twenty

INFORMATION, KNOWLEDGE

156

EARLIER IN THIS BOOK was presented a definition of WISDOM taken from the Encyclopedia of Philosophy published in 1967. For purposes of orientation, it is worthwhile repeating it here – because some of its elements will now be taken apart and examined piecemeal.

"WISDOM in its broadest and commonest sense denotes sound and serene judgment regarding the conduct of life. It may be accompanied by a broad range of knowledge, by intellectual acuteness, and by speculative depth, but it is not to be identified with any of these and may appear in their absence. It involves intellectual grasp or insight, but it is concerned not so much with the ascertainment of fact or the elaboration of theories as with the means and ends of practical life."

On its surface, this definition appears to fit the bill, and also to acceptably prescribe the qualities a Wisdomer should aspire to – if "the means and ends of practical life" are understood as referring to "positive practical life."

Even so, although the use of the term "knowledge" seems clear and appropriate enough, its actual contexts always remain ambiguous, based on the questioning precept of "Who's to say what knowledge is or is not?"

157

About 380 years ago, there appeared on the philosophical scene a since famous and influential philosopher who DID say something about knowledge that perked up everyone ears and intellects.

This was the French philosopher Rene Descartes (1596-1650) who has been credited as one of the founders of modern thought and with being one of the most original philosophers and mathematicians of any age.

He is also credited as originating the concept that "Knowledge Is Power." Well, yes, from one perspective at least. But he couldn't possibly have been the "originator" because something along such lines had obviously existed long before the post-Renaissance period.

What Descartes' words seem to have done, however, was refresh the notion that knowledge directly leads to power, and to establishing it, as having some kind of a higher rank above knowledge that is merely knowledge. Thereafter there was a tendency to examine knowledge only through the lenses of power-value-added.

One of the results of this was increasing interest in the power-value-added parts of knowledge, accompanied by increasing disinterest in accumulating knowledge merely as knowledge per se.

This tendency is still on-going today, in that many researchers cannot get funding for their projects unless they portend power-value-added to existing power, or at least to someone's existing power.

So, like science for the sake of science, knowledge for the sake of knowledge is, at least in the conventional sense, held in low esteem – although there have evolved many Machiavellian subterfuges leading "the public" to perceive otherwise.

158

At first take, it might be thought that knowledge and information are equivalent to each other. This is obviously the case in some instances.

But more basically speaking, knowledge needs to be organized and constructed into forms that can be accepted as knowledge, and this process is always based on eliminating data and information that do not fit with the ultimate knowledge forms achieved.

In high contrast to this, data and information are available all of the time, whether or not they can be fitted into the knowledge-making process. The organizing and constructing of knowledge makes it possible to separate data and information into categories, so as to be able to assemble things into the class they logically belong to.

Knowledge assembling thus takes place at some time AFTER perception of data and information. Even then, if various kinds of data-information cannot be perceived as fitting into some already existing knowledge category that is thought to be logical, then those kinds of data-information are excluded from the knowledge-making process.

To repeat, but in another way, knowledge categories are held together via the logical affiliations of the data-information they contain, but with the proviso that the logical affiliations are either seen to be, thought to be, or can be proved to be "logical" – AND from which the "illogical" can be excluded or eliminated.

Although it may be daring to suggest it, the entire foundations of the modern sciences steadfastly rest upon this "logical" distinction of knowledge building. As many have pointed out, minor and/or major paradigm shifts do not take place in the sciences unless it can be demonstrated that the former paradigm is not exactly or completely as logical as was thought.

Thus, there are discrepancies between knowledge and information. To their credit, the authors of the definition of wisdom quoted above took this discrepancy into account by indicating that although wisdom can include knowledge, it may "appear" in its absence – via "intellectual grasp or insight," or, for that matter, via intuition, telepathy, and clairvoyance, and perhaps via other states of perception that have never been identified.

159

So, it turns out that "information" is more interesting than Knowledge, at least from several viewpoints inclusive of wisdom–making.

Contemporary dictionaries generally define INFORMATION in ways we all take for granted: "The communication or reception of information or intelligence; knowledge obtained from investigation, study, or instruction [i.e., from educational learning]."

But the English term is taken from a combination of Latin IN + FORMA, meaning to PUT or MAKE into a form. In other words, something exists before a language "form" is made via which the pre-formless information can be conveyed and exchanged via the formation of a word for it.

Expressed otherwise, and basically speaking, information is what exists before words are made for it, i.e., words are made after the fact of perceiving information. Thus, information does not originate in the words ultimately made up so as to express it.

This is substantiated by the known fact that different cultures erect different words, the meanings of which can be shown and recognized as referring to the same information.

For example, there are thousands of different linguistic words for water. The meanings all refer to water – and the substance can literally be pointed at in case of linguistic difficulties.

Words can even be formed for things that are insubstantial, such as the intrinsic of all things, and especially the intrinsic nature of life itself.

While these can hardly be physically pointed at, but the meanings of which are commonly inferred and recognized everywhere in whatever language, at least by those who have achieved sufficient "intellectual acuteness" to do so.

160

The definition of wisdom we are discussing indicates that although "intellectual acuteness" may figure in the emergence of it, wisdom "may appear" in its absence.

This is a rather hard nut to crack. But there are at least two implications here.

The first is that "intellectual acuteness" is probably not the same thing as one's intelligent quotient (IQ), because many whose IQs have been measured and tested as average or lower-than have evinced various kinds of "intellectual acuteness" that seem somewhat absent in above-average IQs.

With respect to wisdom, the second implication is that it can "appear" in ways, or from yet wordless sources, that are obviously beyond mere intellectual acuteness, and which quality is thus not necessarily needed (although, to be sure, would be more helpful than mere categorized knowledge would be). We will return to this particular topic ahead.

161

The definition of wisdom also refers to "speculative depths." This is yet another hard nut to crack, for were it not, there would perhaps be much more wisdom.

There is one helpful clue. It seems that we are used to speculating about things, but not so used to speculating about their "depths."

One of the official definitions of DEPTH is rendered as "A part that is far from the outside or surface." In this book, "depth" is herewith daringly reworded as: "A meaningful part that is far from a meaningful outside or meaningful surface."

In English, we have only one word that is equivalent to the reworded definition. PROFOUND – which is principally defined as: "Extending far below the surface; coming from, reaching to, or situated at a depth; all encompassing; complete; insight."

Although the definition of wisdom we are considering indicates that it can "appear" in the absence of "speculative depth," the presence of such would seem very helpful, indeed.

This aspect will also be reintroduced ahead.

Chapter Twenty-One

PRACTICAL LIFE, The

162

THE DEFINITION we are examining ends up by stating that wisdom, and application of it, is specifically concerned "with the means and ends of practical life." So it may be worth knowing how this obviously important concept was and is defined.

The Oxford Dictionary establishes that the term PRACTICAL entered English only about 1604 when it referred to: "Actually involved in the practice of some occupation; having, or implying, value or consequence in relation to action; available or applicable in practice; capable of being turned to account [i.e., profitable in some way]; useful."

At about 1617, these definitions were slightly modified so as to indicate the opposites of the practical – "the speculative, the theoretical, the ideal."

By 1667, another definition was either added or substituted: "Devoted or inclined toward action (as opposed to speculation, etc.); whose knowledge is derived from practice rather than theory; also, having the capacity or ability for action."

At about 1840 was added the idea of "Practical men."

Our present definitions simply reiterate the foregoing ones, implying that the early concepts have not been "advanced" too much.

It should also be noted that our English term is derived from the Greek PRAKTIKOS: "To pass through; to pass over; to fare; to get along; to succeed; to do."

163

As they stand, the foregoing definitions seem

straightforward enough, and that is well and good.

But if one cogitates upon them, they appear, more than anything else, to fall very closely to the categories of reason, logic, and the rational, even if these categories occasionally benefit by being linked together by strong ropes of "common sense" – this latter referring to a human category that has not been included in the formal definitions of the Practical.

It is thus to be wondered why the practical should need "qualities" such as "a broad range of knowledge" (or too broad of it, anyway), or "intellectual acuteness." The definitions establish that "speculation" is one of the opposites of the practical, and so the latter would have no use for "speculative depth," or "intellectual grasp or insight," or, for that matter, intuition, etc.

Such "qualities" are defined, in the Encyclopedia of Philosophy, as attributes of wisdom-making, which, when combined or recombined in different ways, are closely associated with achieving wisdom outputs when they do "appear" with or without them.

But after this is said, then the Encyclopedia's authors of the wisdom definition go on to indicate that its ultimate service is directed to "the means and ends of practical life."

Well, the advocates of means and ends of practical life have not agreed. Indeed, many of such advocates prominent in modernist philosophy, science, and psychology, have insisted that such means and ends are alone achieved via the qualities of reason, logical, and rationalism - and which "qualities" do not appear in the definition of wisdom.

While this discussion could be interpreted as an effort to minimalize the categories of reason, logic, and rationalism, that is not the case – for those categories are important and meaningful and will always be.

Rather, the point has been to light up the apparent fact that there are discontinuities among various human categories of mind and consciousness that, in one short-sighted view or other, have been deemed as opposites to each other, and which "opposites" have artificially but vigorously been given sustaining substance as such.

Chapter Twenty-Two

"WHY CIVILIZATIONS SELF-DESTRUCT" – ALONG WITH THEIR WISDOM AND PRACTICAL LIFE

164

IN THE EIGHTH DECADE of the twentieth century, a man named Elmer Pendell published a small book entitled WHY CIVILIZATIONS SELF-DESTRUCT (1977).

At the time, Pendell was one of the world's foremost population experts who had received many distinguished service awards, and who had received his Ph.D. from Cornell.

Although in his 1977 book he elaborates his arguments and theories in the light of many kinds of social conflicts, his basic hypothesis is quite simple.

Before going into that, it seems advisable to reiterate two of the formal definitions of CIVILIZATION, to wit: "A relatively high level of cultural and technological development; and, to bring to a technically and rationally ordered advanced stage of cultural development." Here is that "advanced" word again.

165

Pendell allows that a civilization can be brought down by aggressive activities of one kind or another – especially when a civilization is in an internally weakened state. But he posits that if a civilization is already in such a state, then its own self-destruction has already begun – and which makes it all the easier for an aggressive civilization to have its way.

Paraphrasing Pendell just a little, the difference between a strong and weakened civilization is its ratio of internal continuities and discontinuities – and when the latter increase so as to overwhelm the former, then zippo, the civilization collapses from within itself.

Something like this has been observed time and again through history, and it is an accepted fact in biology and psychology that when the internal continuities of any organism are internally disrupted by discontinuities, the organism "self-destructs" within itself – taking along with it any advanced state it may have achieved.

166

CONTINUITY is defined as: "Uninterrupted connection, succession, of union; uninterrupted duration in time" which result in enduring "cohesion and coherence," and the whole of which would clearly result in some kind of "serenity" of whatever functions are involved.

So, of course, DISCONTINUITY is defined as "lack of continuity or cohesion."

167

Pendell does not apply his theories to Mankind or Humanity. But the direct implication is that if such, now in process of approaching the outlines of world civilization, do not "move collectively" toward some kind of "advanced" species-wide continuity, then the worst might be insightfully expected – as it is already being pictured in forthcoming gloom and doom scenarios.

However, it can be pointed up that such gloom and doom scenarios have their focus on discontinuities, thereby giving them energetic promotion and hype. Any wonderment as to whatever our human continuities might consist is barely discernable.

It is quite possible to think that the human species has not just conscious but also INNATE continuities, for if not it would have gone down the tubes a long time ago and become extinct – like so many of our past civilizations have.

168

It is now with some enjoyment that this author once more returns to the topic of "advanced" ET civilizations, and which, if they exist, might have had billions of years to become advanced.

Hypothetically speaking, ET civilizations Out There and elsewhere, composed like us of organisms with minds and consciousness, would not have been excused from having to deal with the initial problems inherent in their own discontinuities.

So, it is entirely possible that ET civilizations (once composed of their practical life versions) that were overwhelmed by their discontinuities would remain only as piles and heaps for advanced ET archaeologists to dig and excavate.

Thus, when we wish, if only figuratively so, that advanced civilizations might arrive to save us before we self-destruct, we are basically hoping that they will save us from discontinuities we have not managed to cope with, even in a minimally conceptualized form.

Additionally, although it is seldom expressed anywhere, if advanced civilizations HAVE become advanced, then we would assume that they somehow had obtained wisdom enough to recognize, nurture, and advance their pro-creative continuities – rather than engaging in lascivious fulminations about their counter-creative discontinuities.

Whether referred to as Mankind, Humanity, or some collective whatnot, the human species has numerous kinds of continuities that have endured through time. Without question, the chief of these is human consciousness itself, and the thirst for intrinsic wisdom that goes along with it.

Chapter Twenty-Three

WHAT IS THE FULL SCOPE AND DEPTH OF HUMAN CONSCIOUSNESS?

169

THE FIRST ANSWER to this question is that we don't know. We all live within collective human consciousness, of which our individual components are a part. Yet, after what appears to be at least 8,000 years of recognizable human civilizations, our accumulated knowledge has practically no answers to this important question.

One probable reason for this is that past and present knowledge makers haven't yet "advanced" toward the necessary stage of intellectual acuteness, or speculative depths, that suggests the advisability of filling in answers to this question.

But there are some partial answers, one of which is that the collective of human consciousness per se is NOT self-destructive. If human consciousness was completely or even largely self-destructive it wouldn't have survived much past its own get-go.

Even when it comes to the question of the existence of negative archetypes of the collective unconscious, these are not of innate human consciousness itself, but merely constitute deep rooted memories stored within it based on having collectively, through time, experienced this or that negative event or situation.

In this sense, the collective unconscious could be thought of as some kind of species-innate, self-contained "library" that doesn't use alphabets, words, or numerals for memory-file locating, but instead uses packaged-emotion-images that speakers of any language can recognize and identify.

It is possible to think that the consciousness of even

advanced civilizations elsewhere must also have a collective unconscious of approximately the same sort. And so the existence of packaged-emotion-image "libraries" could be universal wherever mind-consciousness is to be found.

170

There obviously are many ways to begin to examine the fuller nature of human consciousness. One can benefit by considering the distinctions of its continuities and discontinuities. Such would at least work to the benefit of aspiring wisdomers who could use some sort of intellectually acute grasp with respect to this.

As has been discussed, on its surface a discontinuity is something that disrupts a continuity.

The formal definitions of discontinuity imply that discontinuities only interrupt continuities, but of and in themselves discontinuities are not continuous. If they were, then no continuity could remain continuous.

Discontinuities, when they become manifest, carry the intrinsic meaning that they have ends, end points, or will come to an end. Therefore, discontinuities are not endless – being merely disruptive and interruptive of a continuity, which in ITS implicit meaning IS endless, unless, of course, a continuity disappears altogether.

But since everything we know of in the universe, or cosmos, is held together not by discontinuities, but by continuities (often expressed as "laws" of continuity), the utter disappearance of continuities is entirely unlikely in the bigger pictures of all things.

In our human world, negative activities act as discontinuities. But such come and go, and the positive continuities of innate human consciousness get underway again.

171

As but one example of all of this, wars are universally considered as discontinuities disruptive of what would otherwise be the continuity of peace.

Additionally, it is generally accepted that wars come into existence for hardly any other reason than conflicting reality boxes, and which consist of little more than this or that particular or peculiar version of reality.

When wars, as discontinuities, come each to their own end, the vanquished reality boxes also come to an end, leaving the conquering reality boxes yet again to face the emergence of other conflicting reality boxes.

Thus recommences the "play it again, Sam" war theme, which has tended to hypnotize just about everyone, including historians, to the degree that they have not produced any histories of peace itself.

172

As a brief aside, if one more fully contemplates the "nature" of conflicting reality boxes, it is possible to comprehend: (1) that they consist of little more than temporary mind-made versions of reality; but (2) that such versions are temporarily made within a greater mind-consciousness that is a permanent medium for all formats of reality boxes that can be made within it.

Another way of putting this is that greater mind-consciousness COMES FIRST, simply because if such did not first exist, then no versions of reality boxes could manifest within it. First there is always the medium, but which can be shaped this way and that into different formats, ALL of which are temporary expressions within the fundamental medium.

173

As a brief aside, and in the context of this "first-ness," it is worth pointing up that the collective consciousness has numerous archetypes in the collective unconscious, and all of them are symbols of continuity.

Among these is the closed Circle, which, in its most pristine and metaphysical sense, symbolizes All THAT IS, and the "perfect and balanced" symmetry of its continuity.

174

The "Logos" symbolizes the continuity of life-consciousness of the universal divine mind.

The "Egg of the Ureaeus" symbolizes the continuity of what all eggs do as "vehicles" of the continuity of life and life-consciousness.

The "Philosopher's Stone" symbolizes the continuity of the universal "substance" that transmutes base forms into higher ones, with specific reference to transmuting lower order "mind" to higher functioning.

175

Discontinuity can disrupt continuity. But by the term's own definitions, discontinuity is itself discontinuous. Thus, although discontinuity has its own beginning, it has its own end, too.

Discontinuity also has its own archetypes in the collective unconscious, two of which are the thunderbolt and a falling tower or pillar. Another is the archetype of Armageddon – i.e., the energies of opposing discontinuities becoming so great that equally great destruction must result.

There is also the End of Times archetype. Discontinuities can begin ignominiously enough as to be barely noticeable. But when their intrinsic negative energies mount and increase, their ultimate, destructive ends become cognizable, and the End of Times also does, which is why such Times can be predicted as such. This is certainly why individuals focusing only on negative discontinuities, and excluding focus on positive continuities, can end up predicting the End of Times and little else.

But even so, there is still the matter of pro-life continuities. Devotion to an excessive and enhanced thrall of discontinuities can "cloak" these into invisibility almost in the same way that Federation starships can.

As a general rule of thumb, one "sees" only what one focuses on, or wants to focus on, and all else disappears into "invisibility." So, unless one focuses on continuities, one probably will neither see them, nor be able to incorporate them into one's reality box.

176

We clearly have to assume that the duration SO FAR of our species is fundamentally and firmly mounted on innate mind-consciousness continuities that make continuation of human life possible – the basics of which are innately forwarded into each generation down the line and into the future.

There are, of course, physical continuities that are necessary to continuation of existence. But there are also specified innate continuities of mind-consciousness which, taken all in all, are exceedingly different from those of all other biological organisms we know about – except as we might imagine in the case of "advanced civilizations" elsewhere.

If we account for mind-consciousness on a scale from 1 to 10, we will (as has been done in the past, especially in the seventeenth and eighteenth centuries) rate our own at 9 or 10 and rate all other suspected forms of it at 1 or 2.

There is nothing to rate in the intervening area between 2 and 9 – except for a possible 3+ in the case of chimpanzees, dogs, elephants, horses, and camels, etc., who can undergo behavior modification by training.

Even then, there are grounds to suspect that such animals are not so much responding to the training as they are to archaic telepathy of their own, via which they are sensing what humans want of them.

177

Now enters a rather sizeable problem with respect to considering the full scope and depth of human consciousness. We can comprehend, or at least accept, that the 1-3 animal traits are innately heritable through each of the species. We can even accept that our own 9-10 status is innately heritable.

However, we have not a clue as to how or why our 9-10 status came into existence.

This glitch is glossed over by the assumption that it evolved along with our Cro-Magnon physical structures somewhere about 50,000 to (more likely) 35,000 years ago, and which is but a very tiny fraction of Earth's own 4-billion-year-old history.

Skeletal remains of Cro-Magnon people were discovered in France only in 1868 in a rock shelter called Cro-Magnon. Cro-Magnon stood straight and was six feet (180cm) tall. The head was balanced as in modern man, the forehead was high, the brain large, and the chin well developed. Skillfully made flint and bone tools, shell and ivory jewelry, and polychrome paintings found on cave walls indicate a relatively advanced culture.

Cro-Magnon is of the same species as modern man, i.e., ourselves, named Homo sapiens sapiens.

178

But, here is a second glitch. Insofar as is yet known, Cro-Magnon "appeared" intact and complete on the scene without any so far discoverable link to biological structures thought to be Mankind's evolutional predecessors.

Although there is evidence that some of the original Cro-Magnons lived in primitive situations, there is additional evidence that they behaved in ways that correspond to our own mind-consciousness.

For example, they buried their dead with flowers. Perhaps they didn't understand why any more than we today really do, except that it is felt to be appropriate. This, and other similarities (such as making and refining tools) suggest that Cro-Magnon innately possessed a consciousness similar to ours.

It is quite possible that Cro-Magnon, in order to survive the contexts of the Ice Ages in which they appeared, could have developed their innate qualities of insight and intuition, and thus somehow have based their versions of wisdom in them.

We will never know this for sure, of course. But our own mind-consciousness containing the categories of insight, intuition, and wisdom apparently descends from that of Cro-Magnon.

Chapter Twenty-Four

CAN KNOWLEDGE AND WISDOM BE DESTROYED?

179

WHEN WE THINK of human mind-consciousness, we tend to associate it with the "knowledge" that is being manifested out of it.

Having achieved this association, we then tend to think within the contexts of whatever the "knowledge" consists of, and to lose sight of the mind-consciousness behind it.

But it is quite clear that if the mind-consciousness did not first exist, then there could be no production of "knowledge."

We also, in general, think of knowledge (and, sometimes, wisdom) in the ideal, as a sort of metaphysical standard of perfection, beauty, or excellence, or as exemplifying a model for imitation. We also tend to think that the accumulation of knowledge is and has been on-going throughout our history.

If this latter were the case, then we today would have a complete continuity of the accumulation of human knowledge – as well as the continuity of any wisdom that could be deduced or intuited from the whole of it.

180

But we do not have a grip on this continuity, because time and again throughout our history accumulations of knowledge have been destroyed, erased, wiped out.

As two examples of this, when Alexander (the Great) conquered the Persian Empire, he caused its ceremonial capital, Persepolis, including its palaces, libraries, and archives, to be set aflame and burnt to the ground.

When Alexander then "took" Babylon, the libraries and archives of that great ancient city also suffered a similar fate.

In Egypt, Alexander the Great had founded, in 332 B.C., his city called Alexandria, which ultimately became one of the greatest centers in the Mediterranean basin. At the height of its greatness it had two celebrated libraries, one kept in the temple of Zeus, the other in a vast museum.

Together, these were said to have collections containing some 700,000 texts and archives, many of which were even then of great antiquity. A famous university grew around the museum and attracted many scholars.

At the time of Julius Caesar's invasion of Egypt in 47 B.C., large parts of the libraries were destroyed by fire, said to be "accidental." Later, the libraries and their contents suffered extinction when, in 391 A.D., Theodosius I (379-395) (also known as Theodosius the Great) had all "pagan" temples and other structures throughout Egypt razed to the ground and their contents destroyed – this, by the way, not only in Egypt, but also everywhere throughout the Roman Empire, including ancient Greece, Turkey, Italy, etc.

Further along in time, shortly after America was discovered by Columbus in 1492, successive waves of colonizers caused the libraries and archives of the Incas, Aztecs, and other Mesoamerican civilizations to be destroyed.

When in what was to become the United States, European and African settlers brought with them diseases against which the native Indians had no immunity. It is estimated that upward of 60-70 million of the native population were wiped out.

No effort was made to salvage their historical accumulations of knowledge, which, judged as "pagan" or worse, were committed to flames, etc., sometimes along with some of the remaining Indians.

About the only remaining example of native North American accumulated knowledge and history is the Wallam Olum (the "Red Record") covering almost one hundred generations of the American Indian tribes and civilizations, as passed down verbally by the Lenni Lenape (the "Grandfathers," i.e., the elder sages).

The Wallam Olum was first recorded in words and symbols in red paint on wood at some time in the early seventeenth century. However, its authenticity is doubted by many. (See: THE RED RECORD (1989), translated by David McCutchen.)

181

There are two reasons for dragging through these rather dismal foregoing discussions.

FIRST: It seems that conquering nations, as well as other ideological forces that rise into dominance, trash the knowledge of the defeated and replace it with their own versions. So, traditions of historical value and meaning tend to vanish, along with any shreds of wisdom that might otherwise be found in them.

Thereby, any continuity of human knowledge is made discontinuous, with very little being permanently gained in any of the discontinuities, because these will ultimately be replaced by other discontinuities.

Even in our own times, the rise into cultural dominance of the modern sciences and psychologies trashed anything having the smell of "superstition," "myth," and the so-called "irrational" (including insight and intuition), all of which a proper modern individual should therefore have no interest in.

This kind of activity might compartmentalize knowledge into acceptable and unacceptable areas, with social taboos placed between them. But this does not tell us much about the fuller extent of human consciousness out of which all forms of knowledge arise.

Indeed, it is generally admitted that Mankind, Humanity, or whatnot, have produced packaged forms of knowledge for well over 7,000 years, and maybe as early as 35,000 years ago. The modern versions of what knowledge should and should not consist of are barely two hundred years old.

182

SECOND: Since we have now at least hypothesized that "advanced civilizations" might exist in the elsewhere Out There, it could be wondered how they have handled this kind of situation in which various kinds of knowledge are destroyed in favor of other kinds of it.

In other words, it is possible to think that civilizations Out There have NOT become advanced by destroying particular knowledge packages, since an enduring continuity or continuum of knowledge cannot be achieved this way.

We can think that such advanced civilizations have had billions of developmental years to sort out this situation by realizing that any knowledge is part of the wisdom-knowledge continuum – the whole of which needs to be preserved and protected from desecration by less advanced civilizations (such as ours) that permit and justify the destruction of various kinds of knowledge packages.

183

It is difficult to imagine how this preservation-plus-protecting could come about, or what form such repositories or facilities would have to take.

It is possible to theorize that such repositories, and their contents, would somehow have to be made inviolate, invincible, and indestructible. We today of course think that nuclear devices and electromagnetic-pulse weapons will destroy anything. But in science fiction tales and movies, ETs are presented as having "shields" that deflect such kinds of terminal equipment, and many technical experts today suppose that development of such shielding is ultimately possible.

184

After making knowledge repositories inviolate and indestructible, there would still be the question of who would have access to them.

After all, it would not be sensible to permit destructive, or even Machiavellian, types to have access to get special kinds of information that could be used to support their dubious motivational ends, even if such had developed interstellar-travel capabilities.

Ways and means would thus have to come into existence having to do with prejudging who should or should not have access. This would somehow involve seeing behind mere platitudes of good intent, and involve the larger, more pertinent goal of identifying whether states of consciousness behind the platitudes are worthy of being granted access into the greater knowledge continuums. In other words, Trojan Horses would have to be seen into – and denied access.

We have only one word that fits the bill for this kind of "seeing into" – i.e., telepathy, via which we expect that no motivations and intentions can remain undetectable.

On Earth today, this kind of thing is no longer thought of as impossible. Beginning with the advent of lie-detecting equipment, well-funded development of "intelligent machines" to enhance and extend such detecting are well underway.

Earth-based concepts of "intelligent machines" perhaps provide the clue that inviolate repositories of knowledge might, within themselves, have capabilities of assessing the problem of admittance to them. Such machines might even have the capability of cloaking themselves in shields of invisibility. Indeed, knowledge is like that anyway, for we certainly realize, based on actual experience, that lower states of consciousness literally cannot "see" knowledge associated with higher states of it.

185

In theoretically pursuing the "nature" of such whole-knowledge repositories, there would also be the question with respect to what forms their knowledge holdings would be preserved in and stored as.

If such holdings were physical, such as books, documents, papyrus, wood, bamboo strips, metallic, stone carvings, clay tablets, etc., then the bulk of the accumulation would not only be perishable, but through even 10 billion years would require a thousand or more planets as storage space.

This would certainly confound the problem of how to keep knowledge continuums "hidden" from the prying eyes and minds of lesser states of consciousness.

In Earth terms, we so far have only about two ideas about this: some kind of refined electromagnetic (EM) storage and transmission, or photon-light storage and transmission. These two forms are thought to be feasible, but in any event, it is now somewhat understood that the human brain works in the contexts of EM storage and transfer, while consciousness-plus-mind may work within the contexts of photon-light storage and transfer.

186

As stated, the whole of the foregoing is merely theoretical, and we shall probably never know anything for certain about it.

Be that as it may, it is worthwhile pointing up that in the collective unconscious there reside several archetypes that bear some kind of relationship to what has been theorized.

Perhaps the first of these archetypes is represented by human (or humanoid) figures showing oversized heads or brain craniums as opposed to those pictured with dots or small ovals. Representations of both types are variously found portrayed in aboriginal cave paintings and on prehistoric rock pictographs.

We may think of these big-head portrayals as merely "archaic," and therefore meaningless. But in modern science fiction literature and movies, they reemerge with respect to advanced extraterrestrials whose overly large brain craniums signify superior thinking processes, intelligence, knowledge, and wisdom – and the bigger the cranium, the more knowledge stored in it.

There is another archetype that suggests much the same thing, without the necessity of distorting the human head. Images of this archetype are achieved merely by placing a large circle (an archetype discussed earlier) around the head, filling it with some kind of light, so as to portray an aureole extending outward beyond the brain that symbolizes both insightful and radiant knowledge, etc.

Light itself is a major archetype symbolizing knowledge, or awakening of it, and is firmly embedded in the collective unconscious, having symbolized such throughout the world and in all civilizations and societies.

187

There is a "Secret Hall of Treasures and Records" archetype in the collective unconscious. If this archetype becomes even moderately stimulated by reference to the possibility of such a place, it can suddenly pop up on the imaginative and hopeful radars of a great many people – albeit usually more because of the "Treasure" part than the "Records" part.

The "Records" part of course refers to archives of knowledge (once considered a treasure) secreted away, usually to avoid destruction of them, and/or to invisibly hide them during epochs of profane activity.

Mythology is quite populated with such Halls, and there are many legends involving civilizations that, having foreseen then-own coming destruction, secreted or buried them as sort of "time capsules" to be "opened" when times are again appropriate to do so, and when the hidden knowledge will not be misused.

Various legends indicate that Atlantis has its own Hall, as does an ever earlier nebulous civilization. Other Halls are said to reside beneath the Gobi Desert, in mountainous caverns of the High Himalayas (especially in Tibet), in the South American High Andes Mountains, beneath or near the North and South Poles, and even in the American southwest.

Others are said to be beneath the oceans, placed there before the meltdowns of the glacial period lifted the oceans levels to their present depths. Egypt has its own special Hall of Records, said to be beneath or in some proximity to the Great Pyramid. Yet others are said to exist in inaccessible monasteries that, furthermore, are defended, either by physical force or by some kind of telepathic hypnosis, against profane access.

188

Now, before one keels over laughing at such legends, it needs to be pointed up that such Halls frequently appear in dreams, always have done so, and still do today.

While the meaning content of such dreams can remain inscrutable to some, they are otherwise generally interpreted as portending an awakening or connecting to some kind of "hidden" knowledge and wisdom. Sometimes such dreams include images of elderly "priests" or "monks" with long white beards, which reflect one of the major wisdom archetypes earlier reviewed.

Dreams can sometimes refer to physicality of one sort or another. But otherwise it has been accepted, even in ancient times, that they more refer to "psychological" content development, and sometimes to portending higher "spiritual" levels of consciousness.

189

Then there is the Akasa archetype. AKASA is a Sanskrit term essentially meaning "brilliant, shining, luminous." It is the fifth cosmic element, the fifth essence or quintessence, which was called AETHER (or SUBTLE ETHER) by the ancient Greek Stoics. (As discussed, please remember that in earlier Western thought the angel of wisdom is said to be of the fifth rank.)

Some definitions of Akasa indicate that it is not the aether of science, whose own aether is merely one of its lower elements. In the various branches of Buddhism, it refers to the cosmic spirit-substance, the reservoir of Being and of beings.

The Hebrew Old Testament refers to it as the cosmic "waters."

Science, however, being of a lower element, does not refer to it at all, and in demonstrable fact the modern sciences and psychologies have altogether objected to even the use of the term "Aether."

In general, Akasa IS the universal substantial SPACE.

190

AKASA is its own archetype, albeit one of considerable metaphysicality.

From it, however, is derived the archetype of the Akashic Records which denotes a kind of central filing system of all events, thoughts and actions impressed upon an "astral" or "aetheric" plane, and which may be consulted in certain conditions of consciousness.

Throughout all time infinite, events are thought to make an "impression" or "imprint" on the Akasa or subtle Ether.

By analogy, the "Records" reside in what we today might call, in computer lingo, a "zipped file" – which may be opened up and reanimated by "mystics," like a celestial television set.

Several noted inventors of genius such as Albert Einstein and Nikola Tesla (who admitted to being a "mystic" in addition to being a scientist) indicated that their insights originated from some source outside of them.

Both talked of such sources in ways that seem to correspond to the akashic records – and could correspond to hypothetical advanced ET repositories of knowledge continuums in which the continuums are sustained and protected.

PART SIX

WISDOM AND WISDOMERS

Chapter Twenty-Five

WHY WISDOM?

191

THROUGH THE AGES, it has been generally agreed, if only intellectually, that several potentials for wisdom exist in our species, for which archetypes are found in our species collective unconscious.

If it is the case that archetypes are formed because of impact of actual species experiencing, then it would seem that our "archaic" ancestors experienced meaningful epochs of wisdom at some very distant time and place in the past.

This distant time and place is usually thought of as involving only the rather short duration of our species existence on Earth, beginning, it is currently thought, approximately 35,000-years ago.

192

There is an interesting nuance to all of this. Evidence suggests that Earth civilizations have never experienced long and meaningful epochs of wisdom on a continuous species-wide basis. Yet the collective unconscious of our species contains vivid archetypes for it.

Therefore arises the wobbly question as to where and when our archaic species experienced and underwent sustaining wisdom impacts strong enough to have formatted collective archetypes for it.

The implication is that even if wisdom impacts cannot have been formatted because of significant Earth-based experiencing of them, deep memory-images of such impacts nevertheless exist in various levels of the collective unconscious of our species, inclusive of our collective unconscious.

This could point to something that seems ridiculous – that our collective unconscious is older than our physical presence on Earth. This might imply that wisdom-making is also older than our physical presence on Earth. Far out, right?

193

In the contexts of Earth-based frames of reference, evidence substantiates the fact that wisdom-making attempts have occurred throughout our known history.

A greater amount of evidence shows that our wisdom-making attempts have not succeeded for very long in overwhelming our own species-wide tendencies of aggression, war, destruction, and other numerous negative whatnots of equally deplorable or obscene proportions.

Thus arise perfectly understandable questions having to do with what wisdom is good for and what use is it.

Considering the enormous and seemingly bottomless scope of all destructive, mean, despicable, vulgar, destructive, ugly, and non-survival-oriented things, it could turn out that there are no useful answers.

However, it is at least possible, in speculation anyway, to open up discussions for whatever they may be worth to whomever.

194

To get into this, it is necessary to return to the definition of wisdom found in the Encyclopedia of Philosophy. This definition establishes that the application of wisdom refers to nothing else than "the means and ends of practical life."

Of course, there is no doubt that achieving the means and ends of practical life could use a little wisdom. But something about this depends on what one considers the practical life to consist of.

It is practical to provide toilets and sewage systems, and to dispose of raw garbage before it rots and stinks up the place. It is practical to arrange for shelter, clothing, food, and other basic whatnots. It is practical to get along with as many as possible.

Some think that because wars are inevitable, it is practical to prepare for and see them through no matter the costs involved.

Some who have achieved societal power think it is practical to arrange educational matters so as to keep those subservient as ignorant as is practical, and to this dismal end, many think that secrecy is not only practical but also necessary.

Some even think it practical to limit knowledge, even their own, and many think it is practical to obscure information about awareness lest versions of it appear that are superior to their own. Others even think that the dumbing down of human consciousness per se is practical. A listing of such practicalities can go on for pages.

195

As has been referred to earlier, most dictionaries define PRACTICAL as "actively engaged in some course of action or occupation; whatever serves ordinary or material needs."

So, it is generally understood and accepted that "practical" always refers to various kinds of physicality and being actively engaged in some course or occupation within whatever has physical parameters.

There is again no doubt that actively engaging within whatever has physical parameters could sometimes use a little wisdom. But it is far more likely that such could depend on common sense, in which case wisdom would not be too much needed.

196

Most dictionaries have an entry for COMMON SENSE, to wit: "Sound and prudent judgment; the unreflective opinions of ordinary men."

These two definitions are somewhat conflictive in that "unreflective opinions" of ANYONE might not result in "sound and prudent judgment," and so it is rather odd that these two definitions should appear together. (There is also the issue of what "ordinary men" consist of, but there is no urgent need to discuss this here, except to observe that the issue involves little more than lower, or ordinary, social status.)

In any event, arriving at sound and prudent judgment via common sense would seem to have great importance to the practical life. So it is strange to discover there are no organized educational curricula anywhere that might give orientation classes relevant to common sense, and this absence is even the case at the highest university levels.

197

Returning to the wisdom definition we have been dissecting, although the practical life is important, it would seem that serving the means and ends of human life survival per se can take precedence over the means and ends of practical life.

The principal consideration behind this is that if life does not survive, then practical life is automatically deprived of its practical significance.

Beyond any doubt or argument, human life is composed of much more than its practical physical aspects, and without the incorporation of this "much more" we would have no justification for thinking we are anything other than mere "stimulus-response" mechanisms.

Indeed, without this much more we would not even be able to recognize that we were stimulus-response mechanisms.

198

A listing (which has never been compiled) of our much-more-ness would be quite lengthy.

But it is convenient to mention a short listing of our species undoubted possession of intelligence, introspection, pro-creativity, inventiveness, imagination, insightfulness, foresightedness, knowledge discovery and accumulation, prediction, planning, building, modifying all things, mental mobility, empathy, emotional capacities – and, above all, the kind of consciousness within which and out of which all the former can collectively proceed to manifest in ways that often astonish ourselves.

Thus, taken altogether, our much-more-ness is a vastly more complicated affair that is far senior to mere practical life – so far senior that if our much-more-ness did not survive, then neither would we as a species of Man who thinks and knows that he does (Homo sapiens sapiens). Without our much-more-ness, human life would be awful or abysmal, and it is possible that 80 percent of our species might hang themselves.

Chapter Twenty-Six

THE INTELLECT– INTELLIGENCE CATEGORY

199

SOMEWHERE IN THE VICINITY of about a thousand or so years ago, the English language began to separate from a mixture of Germanic and other ones, and eventually came to include the term SPECIES. In its presumably earliest form, it referred to "appearance of outward form." This meaning was applied to groups of things that were seen as similar in nature – such as types of money, animals, wine, perfumes, drugs, personalities, and even ideas.

It was not until about 1600, when the birthing sciences of zoology and biology began to aggregate as such, that the term was applied as referring to "A group or class of animals or plants having certain common and permanent characteristics which clearly distinguish it from other groups."

At about 1711, the term began to include the "human race." At some later point, various categories of classification evolved that permitted separate placement of all life forms according to genus, species, and subspecies. Since Latin was the scholastic and scientific language at that time, all identified life forms received Latin names.

Our own life form was accordingly dubbed HOMO (genus Man), sapiens (species CAN THINK), sapiens (subspecies KNOWS HE CAN THINK).

The double use of the Latin SAPIENS SAPIENS was apparently seized upon to emphasize what was thought to be the greatest trait of the HOMO genus – intelligence doubled, i.e., intelligence that can contemplate on itself, and which, among other things, makes wisdom possible.

SPECIES was eventually somewhat redefined as any related group or population capable of interbreeding and forwarding their traits into their progeny. This definition still holds today, although the science of genetics can now establish what is related to what via detailed genetic analysis.

The bottom line of all this is that our species possesses self-reflecting intelligence and is intelligent enough to know it.

Yes! There is the possibility of certain giggle factors here, in that if human intelligence is intelligent enough to appraise our species as such, it seems that such intelligence should also be intelligent enough to recognize, well, its own stupidity, as but one example.

200

During the latter part of the modern period, INTELLIGENCE was defined as the "Capacity to apprehend facts and propositions in their relations, and to reason about them; mental acuteness; shrewdness; an intelligent being, especially an angel; the basic eternal quality of divine Mind."

INTELLECT was defined as "The power of knowing, as distinguished from the power to feel and to will; the capacity for knowledge; the capacity for rational and intellectual thought, especially when highly developed."

It is thus established that we have (or at least our still on-going species does) an Intellect-Intelligence category somewhere in the sum total depths of our species consciousness.

201

Based on copious evidence, it is now possible to suggest that if our intellects contained ONLY the capacities for knowledge and rational and intellectual thought, then the "having intelligence" ship of Homo sapiens sapiens would have sunk long ago.

In comparison, it seems far more likely that we are still here because of our "power to feel and to will." At any rate, these powers are far more stubborn with regard to survival or surviving than is any kind of mere knowledge or rational-intellectual thought.

202

Since rational-intellectual thought, usually based on some sort of knowledge packages and/or reality boxes, doesn't quite seem to carry the day at various times, it is likely that our innate intelligent-intelligence category might have many more sub-categories, but which have never been identified or accepted as such. With one exception, there is certainly no educational listing of such sub-categories.

The exception is found in, of all places, Roget's Thesaurus of Words and Phrases (1941), under the general heading of "Intellectual Faculties," which, to be sure, few bother to read as a basic educational text.

The Thesaurus offers up synonyms and antonyms and there is no expressed intent to do otherwise. But, after all, synonyms and antonyms are words each of which represents their own category of specific meanings.

The following word-meanings are associated under the heading of "Intellectual Faculties," either as categories of their own, or as sub-categories of the major Intellect-Intelligence category:

Intellect
Mind
Understanding
Reason
Thinking principle
Rationality
Cogitative thinking
Cognitive thinking
Faculties
Senses
Consciousness
Observation
Percipience
Apperception
Mentality
Intelligence

Intellection
Intuition
Association of ideas
Instinct
Flair
Conception
Judgment
Wits
Parts
Capacity
Intellectuality
Reasoning power
Brains
Genius
Ability, and etc.
Wisdom, and etc.
Soul
Inner man
Heart
Heart's core
Ego
Psyche
Pneuma
Subconsciousness
Subconscious
Subliminal self
Seat of thought
Sensorium
Science of mind
Metaphysics
Psychics
Psychology
Genesis
Thought reading
Philosophy of the mind
Ideality
Transcendental faculties
Immateriality, and etc.
Cognizance
Awareness

Realization
Appreciation

Given as the absence or want of Intellect are:
Imbecility
Brutality
Brute instinct
Brute force
Unendowed with reason
Incogitancy
Vacancy
Inunderstanding
Inanity
Fatuity
Thoughtlessness
Not-think
Put away thought
Unintellectual
Unideal
Unthinking
Unoccupied
Irrational, and etc.
Off one's mind
Not to be thought of
Inconceivable
Unconsidered

These listings have been provided for what they are worth to whomever – but aspiring wisdomers should probably take note of their overall content as it relates to understanding various aspects of wisdom-making.

Chapter Twenty-Seven

WHERE DOES WISDOM START UP?

203

IT IS WIDELY thought that wisdom, like knowledge, is based in a process of accumulating information inputs that can be compared, analyzed, made sense of, and judged with accurate foresight in the light of probable positive or negative outcomes.

In this particular aspect, the usefulness of wisdom is linked to whether (1) the probable positive outcomes are worked toward, combined with whether (2) there is desistance of working in the direction of negative ones.

However, wisdom-making activities do not simply plop down with a completely fresh start. Rather, wisdom appears, if it does, within scenarios consisting of which means are underway to achieve what ends. So whether wisdom is useful, or even feasible, depends on means-to-ends scenarios, many of which have gotten underway in the absence of wisdom foresights.

204

One of the subtle implications of this is that wisdom, if it is to exist, cannot really and dependably unfold itself with respect to pre-existing means-to-ends scenarios, many of which would trash its unfoldment, especially if wisdom would represent inconvenient obstacles to them.

As but one example of such trashing, the principles of Machiavellianism (earlier reviewed) hold that "politics" of any kind is amoral to begin with, and so any means, however unscrupulous, can justifiably be used to achieve equally amoral "political" ends. This is the beginning and end of that story.

It surely cannot escape notice that Machiavellian strategies and tactics, fully intending to idealize the unscrupulous, do not start by consulting wisdom. So it is logical that such strategies and tactics would not have any need of wisdom thereafter, or of too much common sense or intelligence either.

205

The ever-ongoing presence of unscrupulous activities, especially those that are powerful plus being bereft of any foresight, makes it difficult to see how any effective wisdom can get going among them.

With respect to THIS difficulty, aspiring wisdomers cannot merely float in idealizing clouds of wisdom that are totally detached from the baleful grubbiness of unscrupulous activities – because such idealizing clouds have no real power within the contexts of what wisdom is supposed to cure or at least diminish.

Powerless wisdom is, after all, powerless – which is to say, possibly entrancing in the ideal, but relatively hopeless in the long run. Indeed, it is this hopelessness that seems to hang over wisdom-making as a subtle cloud of gloom, and if the historical persistence of this gloom cloud is considered, then wisdom is the victim of its own powerlessness.

206

But this is not exactly the case within the collective unconscious of our species, because therein exists a particular archetype that is involved with the issues outlined above.

It is daring of this author to point up this archetype because via the vehicles of reason, logic, and rationalizing it is deemed entirely imaginary, ridiculous, silly, and beyond the pale. But there is no archetype in our collective unconscious that is not somehow founded on experience.

To get into this, the origins of the term WIS + DOM have earlier been examined. The prefix WIS is a variant of WYS, WISS, WIZ, and WYSAR, all referring to the concepts of wise men, philosophers, and sages.

In its early usage, WIZ referred to the same, i.e., wise men, philosophers, and sages, but ESPECIALLY to such who were "highly skilled in their arts." Our term WIZARD is from WYSAR(D), with the D added, but which is now considered obsolete, along with wizards themselves.

One should not start rolling one's eyes just yet, because the contexts of wizardry may to refer to the power element that seems to be lacking in the contexts of wisdomry, as it might be called. To get deeper into this, however, a slight detour needs to be taken.

207

The basic definitions for ENLIGHTEN are given as: "to furnish knowledge to; to instruct; to give spiritual insight to; to illuminate." For reasons that are obscure, the latter definition is considered obsolete.

ENLIGHTENMENT refers to "the act or means of enlightening and the state of being enlightened by imparting or receiving mental or divine or spiritual light."

In its first sense, enlightenment is associated with Knowledge (capitalized) as contrasted to knowledge.

Among other qualities, Knowledge is connected to those of insight, intuition, precognition, metaphysical recognition, experience, and kenning.

KEN, or KENNING, are terms now mostly obsolete (except in Ireland), but once referred to: "The range of perception, understanding, or knowledge," not with respect to seeing physical things and events in themselves, but to insight, intuition, and precognition, etc., and to Understanding that comes from them.

KEN is an Old Norse term, but there are corresponding terms in early Indo-European, Sanskrit, Hawaiian, and other languages.

LIGHT and ENLIGHTENMENT have traditionally been equated with Spirit, and some occultists assert that the superiority of spirit is immediately recognizable by its luminous intensity. Light is the manifestation of the spiritual Intellect, of the seven virtues, and of the emanations from the "Center" out of which the creative forces emerge.

Psychologically speaking, to become illuminated or Enlightened is to become aware of a source of light information, and, in consequence, of spiritual strength.

In any event, in its original definition, "Enlightenment" is an "occult" term fair and square, and always has had superior connotations. However, if one chops off the "divine and spiritual" connotations as the Western Rationalists did, then one ends up with enlightenment, but not with Enlightenment or Knowledge.

208

Returning now to the topic of wizards, they have been defined, in the past of course, as being in possession of "a seemingly magical transforming power or influence," this in addition to their being wise philosophers and sages.

This would imply that such philosopher-sages have, so to speak, moved upward through several strata or ranks of Enlightenment, so as to have achieved absolute transforming power or influence in addition to their already achieved forms of sagacity.

Legends about wizards, of which there are many, convey the distinct impression that they are not to be messed around with, and that anyone truculent enough to attempt to do so should soon head for the farthest mountains lest they be turned or transformed into frogs, pigs, rocks, or some other whatnot.

Furthermore, if an achieved wizard says that thus and so shall not ignore him or seek unscrupulous ways and means to flow around him, then such ignoring and flowing stops.

And that is power, is it not?

209

There are three reasons for having introduced the topic of wizards.

FIRST: Concerning to wisdom, it can come into existence. But if it is not powerful enough to exert actual, not merely theoretical, transforming power or influence, then (like so many wisdom texts do, along with many other kinds of "lost" knowledge texts), it ultimately ends up disintegrating into the "dust" of the ages.

SECOND: With respect to wizards, it can be discovered that there are several archetypes for them in the collective unconscious of our species.

In accordance with the concept of the collective unconscious, such archetypes should not have indelibly imprinted into it unless somewhere in the archaic past, actual experiencing of them and their powers were, well, powerful enough to have imprinted, thereby becoming innate in the collective unconscious,

Such archetypes pop up into consciousness all of the time, principally in the form of myths, in fairy tales, fables, dramas, poetry, literature, and movies, within which they are eagerly understood and appreciated as such.

THIRD: The vast archaic and cultural extent of wizardry can only mean that somewhere in the whole of human consciousness is a "Wizard" category, which might be somehow linked to the wisdom category, since both have many attributes in common.

Chapter Twenty-Eight

WISDOM-ESSENCE, PRODUCTS

210

ONE REASON WHY it is so difficult to determine where wisdom starts up is that we don't know what it IS in its own essence or substance within the greater workings of human consciousness.

For that matter, we don't know what human consciousness is either, and we clearly have not realized the whole extent of it.

For those interested in wisdom, it is important to be quite clear about this, at least for the possible benefit of aspiring wisdomers – those who attempt to make and produce wisdom.

What we call "wisdom" are the products of it, in the form of ideas, concepts, judgments, etc. We can point to these, read about them, and try to apply them, and we can mistake them for wisdom itself.

Literally speaking, ideas, concepts, and judgments "come out" of something that, well, they come out of. In the light of this, it can be said that wisdom originates and produces ideas, concepts, and judgments that we can recognize as such. But we don't know the exact nature of the originator, which should properly be called Wisdom, or at least the Seat of Wisdom-making.

Comparable to the foregoing observations, we do however recognize that the mind produces ideas, concepts, and judgments – and also thoughts, imaginations, illusions, fancies, desires, hopes, sense, non-sense, etc. All of these and more are products of the mind, but we do not refer to them as mind itself.

It is also generally recognized that products of wisdom need to be accurately insightful and foresightful if they are at all to be used as wisdom guidelines.

Thus, it is also generally recognized that products of wisdom are unlikely to be produced from within the mind that admittedly is always noisily cluttered with various kinds of thinking and mental activity that bear no relationship to accurate insightfulness and foresightfulness.

211

This situation was recognized in ancient and modern Eastern mysticism, and wisdom (seat of) is therefore allocated to some presumably higher "enlightened state of consciousness" that is both refined and powerful enough so as not to be cluttered with mental debris.

Something like this has also taken place in the psychologies of the modern West, where wisdom-making (if considered at all) is allocated to the subliminal consciousness, the sub-conscious, the super-conscious, and occasionally to the collective unconscious.

These represent modernist concepts, utilized in attempts (1) to establish what differentiated categories of consciousness are recognizable, and (2) then to assume that those recognized categories constitute the whole of human consciousness.

But the whole of the dimensions of consciousness are still unknown, and so, in more probable fact, there could easily be sectors and categories within the yet unknown that have never been conceptualized, much less identified and understood.

212

The formal definition of "Wisdom" that has been depended on in this book indicates that its products can download from any combination of knowledge, intellectual acuteness, speculative depth, and intellectual grasp or insight.

After having established as much, however, the definition goes on to state that wisdom can "appear" in the ABSENCE of these otherwise useful faculties.

The basic definition of APPEAR is rendered as "to come into sight" in the physical sense of seeing. However, there are two other definitions that more precisely convey what is meant in the definition of wisdom, to wit: "to come into existence; to become evident." Thus, products of wisdom may come into existence and become (self) evident in the absence of the useful faculties pointed up in the definition.

213

Well, now! Are we to think that wisdom products can come into existence and become evident out of NOTHING? If so, then we are more or less talking occult magic in the sense that what appears does so via "an extraordinary power or influence from a supernatural force."

Interventions from a supernatural force are not unheard of within the scope of human experiencing. So they cannot be discounted simply by denying that humans experience them.

But in modernist terms they can be, and still are, scientifically and psychologically discounted because they do not fall into the predictable laws of nature or the natural as SO FAR identified and comprehended.

214

There is definitely a "missing link" in all of this that seems to be based on the modernist idea that consciousness and intelligence are NOT part of nature, the natural, or the universal order of all things.

In any event, there have existed several hundred aboriginal, archaic, and "undeveloped" cultures, as well as some contemporary ones, that were and are in vivid disagreement about this. Just go talk to some contemporary Navaho's, for example.

From very ancient times onward, the basic premise of such cultures held that all things in the universal orders interface and are interactive, including the innate orders of consciousness, intelligence, and awareness, and which could not exist unless they were a full part of the universal order.

215

One of the reasons for the discussions just above is that

even if "supernatural forces" exist in their own right, there still must be in human consciousness innate "receivers" or "receptors" that match up with whatever influence, information, or "messages" are imparted via such forces.

If not, interactive "communication" between them and human consciousness could not take place.

At any rate, the "supernatural" is categorized as such only because its "workings" are not understood.

216

Returning now to the topic of where wisdom starts up, the term ESSENCE refers to "the permanent as contrasted with the accidental element of being; the real or ultimate nature of a thing, especially as opposed to its existence; the property, or most significant property, necessary to the nature of a thing."

As stated in them, these definitions do not apply to what is in existence, physical or otherwise, but to an essence-nature OUT OF WHICH what comes into existence does so.

Obviously, these definitions apply not to things in existence, but to invisible, intangible metaphysical qualities behind or above them, although such qualities may even be meta-metaphysical, etc.

The point being made in the definitions refers to whatever comes into formative existence is After The Fact of the essences they came out of. This is the same as saying that whatever comes into existence are PRODUCTS of the essences that originated them.

217

If all of this isn't difficult enough, there is yet another complexity, for essences are generally held to be INSCRUTABLE which, in its most basic sense, is simply defined as:

"Not readily understood; i.e., enigmatic; mysterious; unintelligible; paradoxical; incomprehensible; inconceivable; vague; obscure; ambiguous; having double or triple etc. meanings; latency; transcendental; unaccountable; indecipherable, undiscoverable; incognizable; inexplicable;

insolvable; impenetrable; illegible; puzzling; baffling; occult; esoteric; abstruse; searchless; beyond one's depth; inexpressible; incommunicable; unutterable; ineffable."

However, products out-pouring from their formative essences ARE scrutable, and can thus be searched for, investigated, researched, examined, deciphered, and made comprehensible.

That is to say, IF one has sufficient "intellectual acuteness, speculative depth, intellectual grasp, and insight" so as to recognize products of essences for what they are and mean.

However, as pointed up in the definition of "wisdom," these sufficiencies may or may not depend on knowledge, and in any event wisdom products can "appear" without the lot of them, including knowledge.

218

The foregoing discussions imply that there is present somewhere within the total scope of human consciousness a wisdom-making essence category that can, of and in itself, outflow and produce into existence concepts, thoughts, ideas, and understandings that can be conveyed and communicated in some objective form, such as words, glyphs, symbols, etc., and perhaps, in some cases, via archaic telepathic unity.

It is easy enough to understand why the products are themselves thought to BE or CONSIST of wisdom, in that they are scrutable and can be examined, deciphered, extrapolated, and made comprehensible.

But the wisdom products are only carriers of wisdom information usually, one might think, emanating from the wisdom-essence category as impressions. Once "received," such impressions, in order to be conveyed, must be converted into some language, and ultimately be fitted into reality boxes that are amenable to them. However, as has been pointed up, there are reality boxes that are not amenable to wisdom, and in such cases THAT is the end of that story.

219

It thus turns out that one can be in touch with wisdom via its products, in which case one can intellectually learn about what the products say.

While there is no doubt that this constitutes an important acquisition of knowledge about wisdom products, doing so may or may not put one in touch with one's own innate essence, Wisdom category, or as it might be also said, one's own innate Wisdom Grand Central Station.

Since the innate wisdom category remains inscrutable, being in touch with it via scrutable means is probably not all that feasible. But the full extent of human consciousness has at least one other innate category that is equally inscrutable in ITS nature.

In the past, even in the archaic past, this innate category has had many different names in many different cultures. Today, it is referred to as the Intuition category.

It seems that behind our conscious awareness of them, inscrutable categories innate in human consciousness can be in touch with each other, apparently having their own inscrutable ways and means of doing so – providing this or that innate inscrutable category has not gone into a latent condition because of lack of nurturing and exercise.

Chapter Twenty-Nine

IS WISDOM–MAKING INNATE IN HUMAN CONSCIOUSNESS?

220

ON THE SURFACE of all apparent matters, it certainly seems that wisdom would not be innate in our species. Although wisdom, as a word, is found in dictionaries and minimal discussions of it in some encyclopedias, no histories of wisdom have been compiled.

Wisdom doesn't figure very large in philosophical discussions. There are no organized educational approaches to it. It is not observed or practiced as a source of basic positive guidelines, and various echelons of activity eschew it altogether.

221

Before throwing the baby out with the bathwater, there are other things to consider.

We accept (more or less and with a few glitches) that "Man is basically good." But no histories of Man's goodness have ever been compiled, and no educational curricula that focus on this goodness have appeared.

And, as already mentioned earlier, if Man's goodness is somehow associated with peace, we can quickly discover that no histories of peace have been compiled, and serious educational curricula focusing on such are totally absent, too. And while there are, and have been, many War Colleges, there are no Peace Colleges.

So, one could easily assume that War, etc., is innate in our species, whereas the opposites of war are not. If war were innate, then war activities through time would eventually enlarge until they were big enough to overshadow the entire species in an Ultimate Mass War made possible by weapons of mass destruction. Having arrived at such an ultimate point, it becomes questionable and dubious whether advanced civilizations Out There would think of us as civilized or, even, as intelligent.

222

We, at least, are quite firm in our conviction that our species possesses intelligence, that it is innate in human consciousness, and thus is handed down through the generations.

It is quite difficult to think that the essential, formative goals of intelligence and of human consciousness are to engineer their own ultimate destruction – because if so, then it is equally difficult to comprehend why they bothered to get started up in the first place.

We can thus think, hypothetically anyway, that the ultimate goals of intelligence and human consciousness are actually based in goals and functions other than engineering their own ultimate self-destruction.

223

The intelligence category in human consciousness has been discussed earlier, and it is possible to further contemplate on that category via one of the attributes of wisdom-making itself which, in the definition of wisdom, is referred to as "speculative depth."

If one of the basic goals of human intelligence per se is to survive as such, then it seems, in addition to its survival-oriented innateness, there will be found in its workings equally inherent faculties involving ways and means to this end.

If survival-oriented intelligence did not have ways and means of identifying the nature of the "rocks," then the prospects of its survival would at least be discontinuous, if not disastrous.

A rather largish "rock" on the road to survival is the prospect of colliding with self-destruction that could come about because survival-oriented intelligence was too stupid to recognize and foresee its existence ahead of time.

224

It does not take too much imagination to realize that survival-oriented intelligence absolutely must have faculties of foreseeing not only counter-survival impedimenta, but also both positive and negative outcomes of activities.

As it happens, this foreseeing kind of thing is also one of the principal hallmarks of wisdom-making. In this sense, wisdom-making could be seen as a subcategory within survival-oriented intelligence. Even so, survival-oriented intelligence could as easily be seen as a subcategory of wisdom-making.

Either way one contemplates this via "reflection" on it, or via "speculative depth," we need at least to hope that innate intelligence AND innate wisdom ARE innate categories somewhere within the whole of human consciousness – for if not, our "gooses could get really cooked" as the saying goes.

Chapter Thirty

INNATE FORESEEING ATTRIBUTES OF INTELLIGENCE AND WISDOM

225

ALTHOUGH IT MIGHT seem a little yearningly wistful, we can at least hope (1) that the innate categories of intelligence and wisdom do exist somewhere within the many folded fabric of human consciousness, and (2) that within them dwell pregnant potentials for intelligence and wisdom far more advanced beyond our average use of them.

In this double sense, it is worthwhile reminding that INNATE refers not just to "what one is born with," but also as "belonging to the essential innate nature of something."

These definitions are extended to include "Originating in or derived from the [essential innate nature] of the mind or the [innate] constitution of the intellect rather than from experience."

In turn, EXPERIENCE refers to "the usually conscious perception of reality or an external bodily or psychic event." "Experience" thus refers not only to what is happening around us, but also to the degree we have conscious perception of it. "Experience" also includes conscious perception of "knowledge, skill, or practice derived from direct observation of or participation in events."

226

There are a couple of adages, not too old but surely shortsighted, one of which holds that we BECOME what we experience. Another confidently holds that we ARE what we experience.

While both of these adages may be somewhat appropriate in certain situations, it might daringly be pointed up that if we BECOME and ARE only what we experience, then it is not quite clear why we need intellect-intelligence or wisdom in the first place – because what we experience would do it ALL for us.

These comments are not at all meant to downgrade the often meaningful importance of experiencing, but simply to point up that without intellect-intelligence or wisdom, we would not know WHAT we have experienced, or what the experiencing means.

Additionally, however, what we do or do not experience can be socially and educationally managed by those who set about doing so as means to one end or another. Such management can also entail establishing this or that experiencing as real or unreal, logical or illogical, rational or irrational, etc., ad infinitum.

So, experience alone does not quite make up the total picture of intellect-intelligence or wisdom, and clearly doesn't make up the entire package of human consciousness per se. To paraphrase Vannevar Bush, the atomic physicist and war equipment manager referred to earlier, if Science is not enough, then Experience is not enough either.

227

The fact that foresight is sometimes significantly present and at other times is notoriously absent clearly suggests that foresight faculties exist somewhere in the whole of human consciousness. In cases of their notorious absence they are "asleep" or have retired into latency, usually, perhaps, because of purposeful nonnurturing or non-use of them.

In the larger pictures of all human activities, there are always many ongoing means and ends whose "workings" depend on the absence of foresight. As but one example discussed earlier, Machiavellian scenarios wish to be untroubled by too much wisdom, and so would not like their workings bothered with too much foresight either, except in very limited versions that flatter their means and ends.

In these and other scenarios, the very best thing is not to nurture foresight anywhere. And so there are no educational curriculums dedicated to orientation, study, and enhancement of foresight. Has anyone ever heard of a class called Foresight 101?

228

In English, FORESIGHT is defined as:

1) An act or the power of foreseeing;
2) An act of looking forward;
3) A view forward;
4) Action in reference to the future.

The first three definitions are "passive" in nature, because merely experiencing or obtaining a foresight does not of and within itself signify too much.

The fourth definition, however, is "active," or at least potentially so, in that if what is foresighted cannot be thwarted or avoided, it can at least be prepared for.

229

In any event, and to move on, in this book we are talking not about this or that "foresight," but about what seem to be inherent foresight faculties in our species, and upon which the workings of the categories of wisdom and intellect-intelligence must, in some sense of validity, depend upon or be linked to.

One difficulty is that the term foresight alone does not give too much of an impression as to the larger dimensions and magnitude of the essence and meaning throughout our species, or throughout our ancient-to-modern societies and cultures.

To help achieve a better grasp on this magnitude, it can be pointed up that the term has many synonyms, each of which has its own special and slightly different meaning, and each of which could be thought of as interactive sub-categories of foresight, intellect-intelligence, and wisdom.

Prevision
Prospicience
Providence
Long-sightedness
Anticipation
Fore-thought
Pre-deliberation
Pre-surmise
Foregone conclusion
Prejudgment
Foreknowledge
Prognosis
Pre-notion
Second sight
Sagacity
Intelligence
Prospect
Expectation
Pre-cognition
Foretaste
Prospectus
Foresee
Look forward to
Ahead
Beyond
"Scent" from afar
Feel in one's bones
Look, pry, peep into the future
See how the land lies
See how the wind blows
Expect
Be beforehand
Predict
Prognostic
Foretaste
Foreknow
Main chance of
Keep a sharp lookout

Forewarn
Prescient
Against the time when
Premonition
Warning
Prophecy
Augury
Foreboding
Omination
Auspices
Sign of
Soothsaying
Kenning
Prefiguration
Portend
Foreshadow
Ominate
Herald
Precursory
Harbinger
Forerunner
Signs of the times
Gathering clouds
Interpreter
Bird of negative or positive omen
Coming events cast their shadows before them
The mountain will bring forth (something)
A weakly built edifice will fall
Power is only temporary
The bubble will burst

Chapter Thirty-One

WISDOM–MAKING AND WISDOMERS

230

"WISDOMER" REFERS to both aspiring and achieved wisdom-makers.

Aspiring wisdomers tend to seek wisdom from sources outside themselves. This is a perfectly logical and rational process to undertake, for it can at least accumulate knowledge about wisdom – and there ARE types of wisdom that can be made out of knowledge.

On the other hand, achieved wisdomers seem to have recognized that a wisdom category already exists somewhere in the manifold depths of their own consciousness, and which category seems to make wisdom all by itself.

There are no really distinct delineations between aspiring and achieved wisdomers, and it should be mentioned that the words and terms being used here have been selected merely as convenient for the contexts of this book.

231

However, achieved wisdomers have been referred to (in the past anyway) as sages, whereas aspiring wisdomers in general have yet to accede to that status. Such status, to be taken seriously, cannot really be self-assigned, but must somehow be recognized and bestowed by others.

During the modern period and down until today, interest in sages fell to an all-time low. Even so, dictionaries continue to define a SAGE as "one, usually a profound philosopher, distinguished for wisdom; a mature or venerable person sound in judgment; one who is sagacious."

It is helpful to note the definitions of SAGACIOUS, to wit: "To perceive keenly; (given as obsolete) keen in sense perception; of keen or farsighted penetration or judgment; caused by or indicating acute discernment."

"Sagacious" has numerous synonyms referring to states of consciousness, some of which are: capacity; comprehension; grasp of intellect; acuteness; acumen; subtlety; due sense of; depth; profundity; enlarged views; nimble-witted; unprejudiced, unbiased; unbigoted; unperplexed; unwarped; undazzled; etc.

It can be noted that "enlarged views" obviously means being in touch with bigger pictures, rather than being confined within smaller ones.

It can also be noted that "knowledge" and "knowledgeable" are not given as synonyms for "sagacious," perhaps because knowledge can be thought of not as a state of consciousness, but as a commodity that can be managed this way or that, even by Machiavellians.

232

To help enlarge upon the concept of wisdom-making, it is worthwhile, and for the last time, to reiterate the definition of wisdom we have dissected, but slightly amending it here and there:

> "In its broadest and commonest sense, wisdom denotes sound and serene judgment regarding the [positive] conduct of life [and the survival of ALL of its positive elements, practical and otherwise]. It may be accompanied by a broad range of knowledge, by intellectual acuteness, and by speculative depth . . . and by intellectual grasp or insight . . . but it is not to be identified with any of these and may appear in their absence."

It is to be noted that reason, logic, and rationality are not mentioned in the amended definition. But even so, the combination of sound and serene judgment, a broad range of knowledge, intellectual grasp and acuteness, speculative depth, and insight seem to exemplify a potent package.

So, there could be little doubt that various kinds of wisdom are made and produced out of this package, but which may or may not enjoy various levels of sagacity.

233

The definition goes on to state that wisdom "is not to be identified" with any one or any combination of the elements of the possibly potent package because wisdom "may 'appear' in their absence."

Thereafter, the definition does not go on to address how this "appearing" can take place.

The most plausible reason for this is that the compilers of the Encyclopedia of Philosophy did not know how that appearing comes about, but they nevertheless had grounds for making the statement – which grounds, however, are nowhere elucidated anywhere in the Encyclopedia's eight volumes.

So, we are sort of left on our own to theorize – one plausible theory being that there exist within the whole of human consciousness various attributes and functions that transcend all of the elements in the otherwise possibly potent package.

234

What these transcending elements consist of should not be avoided or left in the fogs of paradoxical mystery, simply because in the English language there is easily found a collective term for many of them – INTUITION, which is talked about all of the time, and about which many books have been written.

There is a slight glitch, though. Although people seem to recognize intuition when they see it, and although books have been written about it, it seems that few have actually read and contemplated its dictionary definitions.

INTUITION: "Immediate apprehension or cognition; knowledge or conviction gained by intuition; the power of faculty of attaining to direct knowledge or cognition without rational thought or inference; quick and ready insight."

Also, INTUITIONISM: "A doctrine that there are basic truths intuitively known; a doctrine that right or wrong or fundamental principles about what is right or wrong can be intuited."

Well, now! Did we just trip across one of the small-print bottom lines of wisdom?

235

In the combined contexts of the two definitions above, it now appears that wisdom has at least two bigger picture facets.

For clarity, the first type of these focuses on "basic truths, knowledge, and cognition that intuitively appear without rational thought or inference." This seems to be the most popular type of wisdom discovery, at least within the contexts of wisdom searching and learning.

And, for additional clarity, the SECOND type is said to be involved, in the intrinsic sense, with intuiting "fundamental principles" about what is right or wrong."

Well, distinctions between right and wrong have their "basic truths" too, and the intrinsic meaning of something IS the actual "basic truth" of it.

236

For example, the intrinsic meaning of "wrong" is that it is not really the thing to do or proceed with, largely because the "Way" of the wrong will, by its own definitions, at least eventually devolve into some sort of dismal situation, probably accompanied by woes, regrets, and assortments of destruction – from which, if large enough, we hope that advanced civilizations will arrive to save us from.

Definitions for WRONG are given as: "An injurious, unfair, or unjust act; something immoral or unethical, especially principles, practices, or conduct contrary to justice, goodness, equity, or law; harmful action or conduct without due provocation or just cause; the state of being mistaken or incorrect."

Although these definitions can be applied to any number of situations, it can be noted that they are relatively mild in that they give no hint of what results from the wrong.

Additionally, the phrases of "resulting because of lack of foresight" and "resulting because of lack of intuition" could have been inserted into the definitions to give them a slightly larger perspective.

237

At any rate, the second type of wisdom-making is not that popular, even at the individual level, much less at the social level in which Machiavellian games are always underway, the proceedings of which don't even need the first type of wisdom-making.

There is one significant implication to be derived from this general situation.

Let us think than an aspiring wisdomer can make enough wisdom so as to be able (by any means possible) to discern between intrinsic right and wrong and their equally intrinsic outcomes.

Even so, it will thereafter require volumes more of farsighted wisdom involving how to actively apply them to the world of ongoing human affairs.

As all things stand in the human world, the chances are quite good that aspiring wisdomers could also end up hoping that advanced civilizations will arrive rather sooner than later.

PART SEVEN

"TIME" FACTORS AND WISDOM-MAKING

Chapter Thirty-Two

DIFFERENT KINDS OF "TIME"

238

ONE TRADITIONAL IDEA about wisdom is "Doing the right thing at the right time."

While this makes sense overall, on average most of the effort to do so will be focused on trying to figure out what the right thing is.

During the many years this author researched the topic of wisdom, he generally agreed with the foregoing traditional idea. However, he was rather surprised when he came across the saying of President Teddy Roosevelt, i.e., "Nine-tenths of wisdom is being wise in time."

Dang! In time for WHAT?

In time for what is happening? In time for what's going to happen? And so forth. Well, Yes – and No.

239

To get into this, it is worthwhile establishing that what we refer to as "time" is basically not understood, and, as well, the exact reasons why are themselves not understood.

At the cutting edges of advanced physics and astrophysics, for example, that thing we call "time" seems either to change its contexts or patterns, or to evaporate altogether, or to merge with cosmic forces the nature of which exceed Mankind's collective knowledge and intellectual perception as so far formulated.

What we do understand in general about "time" is that its progress and passing can be intellectually sequenced or dated according to various means and ways and useful standards.

For some time now, "time" has been sequenced according to Earth's rotation and annual orbital motion around the Sun, our central star existing near the outer fringes of our local Milky Way galaxy.

This concept of "time" has become universal on Earth and is measured by the passing of clock hour/minutes, and by calendars set up with respect to the 365 or so twenty-four-hour days it takes for Earth to make a complete orbit around the Sun, and which we refer to as a solar "year."

It is thus that all those living and managing their lives by clock "time" are guided by it, to the degree they are trapped within it and within calendar "time," both of which recede, proceed, and advance in an orderly and intellectually predictable fashion.

There is, however, a slight bump with calendar "time," because the first general idea about it is that it has to begin somewhere. As long as Earth's rotation and orbit around the Sun do not change, then there is no problem with the continuity of solar "time." But calendar "time" constitutes a different matter altogether since it involves locating a point to begin counting from.

This has historically resulted in many different versions of calendar "time." In general, it seems that calendar makers like to base calendar beginnings on an event that to them holds special meaning and relevance.

Thus, there are on-going calendars whose start up points are based on the birth-event of a personage whose chief characteristic turned out – as it NOW must be pointed up – to consist of positive-making manifold elements of inspired and inspiring Wisdom.

Chapter Thirty-Three

"TIME" VERSUS TIMING

240

THERE ARE OTHER kinds of calendar "time," which do not have their focus on "time" per se but on TIMING.

Chief among these is calendar timing based on the four annual seasons and the equinox and solstice points via which the inclination of Earth from north to south and back again could be established to help in predicting seasonal changes and what needed to be done in practical advance preparation for them, such preparations being thought of as a form of wisdom.

In the distant past, no one could merely depend on day-to-day weather conditions to determine when the timing of spring would actually be at hand. The Inclination Calendar of timing is still with us, albeit not as functional in practical matters as it once was.

From Earth's Inclination Calendar emerged the all famous Zodiac Calendar with its twelve signs – from which the astute might predict various changes in general environmental, animal, and human behavior, and which, if successful, was considered a form of wisdom.

It is no longer understood why the ancients world-wide developed an interest in observing the calendar timing motions of the planets, or why they attributed certain effects, auspices, and forewarnings to them that were held to be predictive SIGNS. If this was successful, it was again taken to be a form of wisdom.

What is known, however, are the long-enduring objections to this kind of thing, objections based on the once favored astronomical theory (taken as fact) that the planets were too small and physically too far distant to have effects on Earth.

What has become recently understood, however, is that that

certain planetary configurations seem associated with various kinds of solar eruptions, and these can at least somewhat be forecast as the configurations move into place. It is also understood that certain kinds of solar eruptions can interfere with electromagnetic communication systems here on Earth, sometimes to a serious degree.

Thus, one thing (planetary configurations) seems to "cause" another thing (solar eruptions), which in turn "cause" another thing (electromagnetic difficulties) here on Earth – the correct figuring out of which is at least an attribute of wisdom-making. So it seems that small and even distant things often can and do start up larger and even awesome effects.

In any event, planetary motion timing calendars are still with us, not only within astrology (where they are referred to as ephemerides), but also in nautical almanacs used worldwide by all kinds of sea and ocean-going types.

241

So, "time" is not just a thing in itself, not just a singularity that can be referred to as an IT, but rather something that is far more complex, having various compounded multiplicities.

Fortunately, this is somewhat confirmed via the NEW COLUMBIA ENCYCLOPEDIA (1975), for its entry for TIME begins as follows:

"TIME-sequential arrangements of all events, or the interval between two events in such a sequence. The concept of time may be discussed on several different levels: psychological, philosophical, physical, and biological. As a practical matter, clocks and calendars regulate everyday life. Yet at the most primitive level, man's awareness of time is simply his ability to distinguish which of any two events is earlier and which later, combined with his consciousness of an instantaneous present that is continuously being transformed into a remembered past as it is replaced with an anticipated future.

"From these common human experiences evolved the view that time has an independent existence apart from physical reality. The belief in time as an absolute has a long tradition in philosophy and science. It still underlies the common-sense notion of time. Isaac Newton, in formulating the basic concepts of classical physics, compared absolute time to a stream flowing at a uniform rate of its own accord.

"Efforts to localize time sense in specialized areas within the brain have been largely unsuccessful. In man, the time sense may be connected to certain electrical rhythms in the brain, the most prominent of which is known as alpha rhythms at about ten cycles per second. Apart from purely scientific questions, the accurate measurement of time by establishing accurate time standards poses difficult technological questions."

And, as it might be noted, poses difficult wisdom-making questions as well.

Chapter Thirty-Four

THE SENSES, SENSING, AND MAKING SENSE OF THINGS

242

GENERALLY SPEAKING, if and when the concept of "time sense" enters into consideration, interest and attention usually will focus on the "time" part. The general assumption here seems to be based on the idea that if we learn more about time, then we might sense more of it. The "sense" part seems to be taken for granted and so it appears to need no further examination or inquiry.

(Please don't confuse this observation with being or becoming "sensitive to," which is an entirely different matter with respect to time sense per se. The reason is that "sensitive to" can range and fluctuate along a scale beginning with none or very little increasing upwards to a whole lot depending on individuals and topics involved.)

So, in commencing discussions about time sense (which is an important element in wisdom-making) one must first drag through considerations about what is meant by "sense." This might not be necessary if there existed a basic educative curriculum that included, say, Human Sensing Systems 101.

But alas! In the same way that there is no basic Human Awareness Systems 101, there is no basic or even introductory Human Sensing Systems 101 – and, as well, who has ever heard of Time Sense 101?

243

SENSE has three generally accepted definitional parameters, i.e., as a noun, as a verb, and as in "making sense of something." All three definitional parameters have important interacting implications to wisdom and wisdom-making. Indeed, one can wonder what examples of "wisdom" would be like in the absence of sensing systems and making sense of something. We have only to look around to observe various such examples.

Definitions of SENSE, as a noun, are usually given in the context of SENSE ORGANS. These are defined as: a bodily structure affected by a stimulus (as heat or sound waves) in such a manner as to initiate a wave of excitation in associated nerve fibers that conveys specific impulses to the central nervous system where they are interpreted as corresponding associations."

"A bodily structure" is sometimes referred to as a RECEPTOR, i.e., "a cell, or group of cells, that receives stimuli – a receiver, a sense organ."

Another official definition of SENSE as a noun is given as "faculty by which external and internal stimuli are conveyed to the brain centers where they are registered as sensations.

The four commonly known special senses (sight, hearing, smell and taste) are concerned with the outer world, and external stimuli are received and conducted by sensory receptors concentrated in the eye, ear, olfactory organs [in the nose], and the taste buds [in the mouth]. The so-called somatic senses respond to both external and internal stimuli."

Whee! So far, so good, right? However, there are some glitches involved.

244

FIRST, for reasons inexplicable, the FIFTH commonly known special sense (that of touch) is not referred to but is defined as: "the special sense by which pressure or traction exerted on the skin or mucous membranes is perceived."

SECOND, the term SOMATIC is defined as: "Of, relating to, or affecting the body, especially as distinguished from the germ plasm or the psyche." Did you get that?

Well, if not, GERM PLASM, otherwise known as GERM CELL, refers to "an egg or sperm cell or one of their antecedent cells," i.e., predecessor cells that unite together to form egg and sperm cells. One of the implications here is that egg and sperm cells are NOT parts of the somatic-physical body.

In modern terms, there are numerous problems as to how PSYCHE should be defined. It is an ancient term that seems to refer to the preexisting vital Life-giving energies that animate and are inherent in human beings – as contrasted to their purely physical and material organisms, but around which such organisms are patterned and built.

The modern sciences, and most of the modern philosophies, objected to the existence of PREEXISTING vital Life energies. So, the term PSYCHE was otherwise defined as "soul, self, mind" – the actual constituents of which are, to say the least of it, not entirely understood, and some aspects of which do not altogether seem vital, Life giving, or life animating.

Please note that TWO definitions of SENSE as a noun have been provided above. The first simply refers to SENSE ORGAN as "a bodily structure."

In the second definition, however, this has been replaced by the term FACULTY that principally refers to: "a natural inborn ability, power, or capacity; also, one of the inborn powers of mind formerly held by [and still held by some] psychologists to form a basis of all mental phenomena."

245

Now, there are some rather large and important distinctions to be recognized between "a bodily structure" and "natural inborn faculties" that might serve as "a basis of all mental phenomena." In some cases, the margins between faculties might be quite narrow, largely because bodily structures are inborn, too.

But in the contexts of this book, can it be thought that wisdom and wisdom-making arise from bodily structures alone? The production of wisdom is, in its first instance at any rate, more clearly a compounded product of innate faculties, ability, power, and capacities.

Such faculties can surely benefit from, and be supported by, what is sensed via bodily structures (receptors), and it would be foolish to think otherwise.

But at some point, making sense of whatever data or information is provided by bodily structures can be seen as a process that TRANSCENDS the bodily structures, while such transcending plops one right into the middle of what we call Intelligence, the ostensible fulcrum within which the processes of Making Sense are, well, made.

And this, as well, plops us into the definition of SENSE as a verb, and into the wobbly situation of making-sense-of.

246

As a verb, SENSE (i.e., to sense something) is very briefly defined in most dictionaries as: "to perceive by the senses; to become conscious of (something)." End of story, right? Not so.

For starters, "to become conscious of (something)" is the end product of a complex series of subconscious or unconscious antecedent nervous system processes that sensed "signals" have to negotiate in order finally to emerge into the neo-cortex of the brain where the signal sensations are "recognized" and then consciously perceived as such. If the sensed signals do not enter into the neo-cortex, they are, simply put, not sensed.

Advanced research along these lines has established that in each and every minute an immensely astronomical number of information bits do enter through our whole-body receptors.

Additionally, during the last fifty years, advancing bio-neurological researchers have discovered that our neurological systems possess a gigantic number of micro-receptors, the result of which is that it is thought that every cell in our bio-bodies act as some kind of a receptor, including the cells in our bones.

247

To make a long story somewhat short, after the billions of information carrying "signals" have been "sensed" by appropriate receptors and converted to electronic bits, the electronic bits are then forwarded into the nervous system, the central processing organ, that is so far mainly thought to be the brain.

Along the way, and believe it or not, the electro-signals undergo certain pre-conscious categorization processes, one of which consists of comparisons to surface memory and deep memory storage. If no memory fits are found, the signals are simply "thrown away," and that seems to be that. If memory fits occur, the signal bits are then organized into categories of weak or strong quantitative and qualitative importance.

Although the weak signals might stimulate certain subconscious activity, they are not strong enough to enter into the cognitive cortex. Even some of the strong signals, especially if they are qualitative ones, might not either.

Whatever signals manage to "punch through" into the neo-cortex are then, and only then, sensed and perceived by conscious awareness. So there is sensed, and then there is SENSED.

The most astonishing and even unbelievable aspect of all of this is that while the sum of our millions of receptors are sensing millions of data bits per second, only about fifteen to thirty of them emerge or cascade into cognitive consciousness in that second. And from these few are constructed what we refer to as our present NOW. (For more details about all of this, see THE USER ILLUSION: CUTTING CONSCIOUSNESS DOWN TO SIZE published by Tor Norretranders in 1998.)

Chapter Thirty-Five

THE SENSE OF DANGER

248

THE READER might be wanting an example of "qualitative signals" that might emerge into the neo-cortex and be cognitively sensed for what they are.

As established earlier, most dictionaries give two brief definitions for "to sense," one of which is "to be or become conscious of, for example, DANGER."

This is almost entirely a qualitative factor usually attributed to some kind of high-stage deduction, intuition, or foresight that transcends otherwise standard or localized forms of reason and logic. This qualitative factor is also full part of wisdom, for if wisdom cannot sense danger, then its value decreases accordingly.

It is seldom pointed up that the sensing of danger consists of two parts or facets. The SENSING of it is more or less in the present NOW – with the danger ITSELF being in the immediate future, even if only a few seconds or minutes are involved.

More precisely put, the sensing precedes the danger itself, which clearly implies that "time" has been transcended so as to sense the danger before it actually comes about. Here, then, is an example of the transcending time sense that very many have experienced.

249

There is yet another factor involved in this kind of thing, one so subtle that it is likely to be missed if it is not pointed up.

Whatever composes the cognitively recognized sense of danger has already been subconsciously "made sense of" and "understood" as such before the sense itself can emerge into cognitive consciousness. If such were not the case, then we would never cognitively experience a sense of danger except via conscious processes of reason and logic.

In that a case our conscious selves would consciously have to undertake the laborious conscious processes "of making sense of" whatever might be involved – and the proceedings of such would of course depend on what we are already conscious of.

This process can often successfully happen, of course. But deep and serious dangers often emerge from factors and sources we don't consciously know about, and so we can't incorporate them into our conscious reason and logic processes to begin with.

Something like this has been consciously understood for a very long time.

Indeed, one of the major functions of any intelligence organization (the present CIA for example) is to find out whatever is not known in order to incorporate the implications of it into their conscious reason and logic processes, so as, in turn, to make sense of them before whatever might happen – which simply implies a certain acumen of time transcending or time projecting, in order, hopefully, to make sense of them and be wise in time.

So, as Teddy Roosevelt noted, "Nine-tenths of wisdom is being wise in time." If this works out, then one has demonstrated some kind of wisdom.

However, Roosevelt's saying could be extended just a tad to read: "Nine-tenths of wisdom is being wise in time for WHEN something will happen."

Chapter Thirty-Six

WHEN-NESS

250

THE CONCEPT of "when-ness" might at first be a little difficult to take on board, i.e., to take into one's knowledge networks and reality box frameworks. The most probable basic reason for the difficulty is that "when-ness" doesn't exist as a word, and, second, the term "when" is always used in conjunction with "time."

This is certainly okay – if one is managing life within some kind of clock-time-calendar frame of reference.

And although everyone uses the term "when" all of the time it is not thought of as having a noun form. It is generally thought of as a conjunction used in connection with describing "at or during the time that" something did or did not happen, or what will or will not happen.

Something that does or does not happen can, of course, ultimately be dated in conformity with various artificial time measuring and counting systems. But the "when" of things happen when they do, and do so irrespective of "time" measuring systems and artifices.

Another factor involved is that although WHAT happens or not is interesting, the WHEN of the happening has always been considered of first importance. This is at least somewhat supported by the stark reality that things happen WHEN they do or will. And that IS that, end of story. Thus, and in recognizable fact, the when thing not only transcends but defies all and any artificially designed time counting and measuring systems.

251

As has been discussed earlier, there are very many clock

time frames of reference, and so a question can arise with respect to how all of these came into existence.

This automatically leads to a second question (one of exceeding importance to wisdom and wisdom-making) having to do with what comes first clock-time-calendar frames of reference, or human consciousness.

Well, it seems that human consciousness exists first. If it didn't, no clock-time-calendar frames of reference would be invented, designed, and then perceived as such.

This suggests that clock-time-calendar frames of reference are artificial constructions that are perceived as being useful in various kinds of contexts, depending on the degree of intelligence utilized to identify and appreciate different contexts in which "time" can be reckoned, measured, and counted.

Since there are very many such contexts, there are likewise very many clock-time-calendar frames of reference that give "time" to whatever is being reckoned by each of them.

252

Another definition of "time" is found in the New Columbia Encyclopedia (1975), to wit:

"TIME, sequential arrangement of all events, or the interval between two events in such a sequence. The concept of time may be discussed on several different levels; psychological, philosophical, physical and biological." And etc.

On its surface, this definition seems to make adequate sense, except for a few little examined wobbles: i.e., that psychological "time" and biological "time" are more or less qualitative, while physical "time" is quantitative.

Philosophical "time," whatever it might consist of, can easily be recognized as versions of human thinking seeking somehow to transcend the concrete.

253

In the definition above, please note the phrase ". . . the INTERVAL between two events . . . in a sequence."

The standard modern definition of INTERVAL is given as "a space of time between events or states: a pause." It is the case that "time" between events, etc., can be measured, but mostly only in a passive, static, intellectual, or academic way so to speak.

If the phrase is slightly reworded as ". . . a space of TIMING between events or states," then we are plopped into an entirely different ball game.

The standard and entirely workable definition of TIMING is given as: "selection for maximum effect of the precise moment for beginning or doing something."

There may at first be a slight confusion here because a precise timing moment can also be dated to an extensive variety of artificially established clock-time-calendars, and, as well, an event can be assigned a clock-time-calendar date, but usually only AFTER it has happened or in some way has been FORESEEN or FOREKNOWN.

254

The distinctions made above with respect to the strategic differences between artificially measured "time" and TIMING, lead to a pert and now prominent question: Can we think, for example, that psychological, philosophical, biological, and physical processes actually watch and consult clock-time-calendars in order to select "the precise moment for beginning or doing something?"

Any answers to this prominent question will probably correspond to whatever frames of reference are being utilized by this or that reality box, and it is a full part of wisdom-making to take such into account.

But even so, there is the very old wisdom adage that "all things happen in their own "time," and do so with their own sense of TIMING. There is even an old wisdom adage that supports this: "QUE SERA SERA – what will be will be," when it will be.

255

While artificially constructed clock-time-calendars are functional insofar as they prove to be, there are many phenomena and processes that apparently have their own inherent or innate timing sense – and which TRANSCEND all of the clock-time-calendar systems that might artificially be designed via the intelligence category innate in human consciousness.

If one studies enough of the history and teachings of wisdom sages, it can appear that one of the sum central messages of the whole is to find out, perceive, and work in accord with what IS – versus what one thinks (usually with some confidence) one perceives.

The latter is, of course, simply a matter of prevailing reality-box problems that come and go.

But the former is a problem having its central focus on problems of awareness, identifying and then transcending them by increasing one's parameters of awareness.

It is easy enough to think that in human consciousness overall there is an innate awareness category that somehow underwrites the very existence of our species.

Indeed, what would we be like if we did not have innate and highly specializing awareness potentials?

As it is though, like the innate wisdom and intelligence categories, the awareness category can be dumbed down for any number of artificially induced reasons, but mostly for various reality box conveniences that discourage transcendence of them.

It can be seen, or at least sometimes intuited, that the innate awareness, intelligence, and wisdom categories must somehow work in tandem in order to achieve an optimization of "selection for maximum effect of the precise moment for beginning or doing something!"

So, somewhere in the whole of human consciousness must exist an innate timing sense (which could even include "time" sense), one of whose principal functions would be to transcend artificial whatnots otherwise erected by that questionable factor, the Mind.

Chapter Thirty-Seven

TIMING

256

AS DISCUSSED ABOVE, and now usefully repeated, the definition of TIMING is given as: "selection for maximum effect of the precise moment for beginning or doing something," and,  for that matter, for changing something, becoming aware of something, having cognitions, insights, intuitions, foresights, and undergoing illuminating qualitative states of consciousness.

As also already discussed, among many other processes that could be mentioned, biological, psychological, philosophical, and physical processes and phenomena also have their internal timing sequences that activate in the sequences they do – and which do not first consult clock-time-calendar frames of references in order to identify precise moments for beginning or doing what they do.

It was also mentioned that human consciousness existed before humans began intellectually to recognize the usefulness of clock-time-calendars, artificially designing various kinds of them that were useful for certain purposes meaningful to them.

From these considerations, it can only be thought that natural processes are based upon some kind of innate sequence timing having to do with progression and/or decline intervals.

This kind of thing is recognized here and there, but the usual way it is expressed is as sequencing from point A to point B, from point B to point C, etc.; or from point 1 to point 2, from point 2 to point 3, etc.

However, one is permitted to wonder if, say, biological timing uses alphabets and numerals to recognize and enumerate the sequencing and intervals of their timing.

257

There is yet another point to be made by examining the accepted definition of TIMING – "selection for maximum effect of the precise moment for beginning or doing something."

The phrase "selection for maximum effect" actually has a slight ambiguity within it having to do with "selection [of what] for maximum effect," and without the "of what" part, the term "selection" remains slightly ambiguous in that it could have direct or indirect reference to just about anything.

It seems that this slight ambiguity is noticed, whether consciously or subconsciously, quite frequently, and, in English sentence formulas at any rate, is smoothed over by adding a term of reference that indicates what the selection refers to.

Thus, in the contexts of TIMING, its definition might be amended to read: "selection of a time for maximum effect of the precise moment for beginning or doing something."

But as has been discussed, "time" becomes recognizable only via artificially designed clock-time-calendars that count points and intervals between what is being counted.

Even if the capacity to artificially design clock-time-calendars might be an inherent capacity within intelligence-making overall, it can still be thought that if time sense and timing sense are innate and inherent within consciousness, then they proceed with, well, their own inherent time and timing sense. This much in the same way that natural biological timing, philosophical "timing, physical timing, and psychological timing do.

258

If all of this seems totally confusing, don't blame your intelligence faculties. There are two principal reasons for the confusion: that "time" can only be measured and counted via some artificially designed system to do so; and that there is an intellectual tendency to utilize and lavishly superimpose the word "time" to cover all the bases of what can be perceived and experienced.

This is to suggest that the word "time" may not be the applicable frame of reference with respect to phenomena and processes that do their own thing if and WHEN they do, and within their own sense of timing, so to speak.

It is accepted that "time-sense" is innate in human consciousness, that is to say, basically inherent. But it seems that this inherent "time-sense" existed long before any of the known artificial calendars were produced that mark out periods of time. In this sense, thinking in terms of inherent timing-sense is probably more pertinent. Indeed, in the absence of time-clock-calendars, one can easily have a sense of timing about the when of things. This kind of thing occurs all of the time, in dreams, visions, and even in altered states of awake consciousness.

259

It can certainly be acknowledged that biological and mental processes, for example, do their thing WHEN they do, and seemly within the contexts of their own inherent timing agendas.

Somewhat echoing the venerable Chinese sage, Lao-tsu, of about 2,500 or so years ago, it seems that all things have what might be called a WHEN-NESS potential, for if not then they would stop.

Everyone everywhere wants to know the WHEN of things, so, here is yet another amended definition of TIMING – selection of a WHEN for maximum effect of the precise moment for beginning or doing something.

Chapter Thirty-Eight

"MIND-MADE" WHEN-NESS

260

IT IS WIDELY ACCEPTED that some full part of wisdom is to deduce, fore-think, predict, or foresee not only what will happen but when it will, ostensibly to prepare for it in this way or that – or, in  trenchant cases., simply get out of the way and head for the hills. If this works out well, wisdom has done its thing.

If the outcomes of all things were easily deduced or foreseen, then the whole of what is involved would be a piece of cake.

Even so, something would depend on whether the timing of things could easily be deduced and predicted not only with respect to "the precise moment for beginning," but also whether the beginning might be plotted to some clock-time-calendar system.

261

As it has happened in the scheme of all things, all self-regulating processes have their own sense of timing. Many such processes carry on their sequential activities without due reference to any clock-time-calendar measuring devices.

262

It is the case that if such self-timed sequential activities follow some kind of given order that can be studied and identified, then a range of predictability can be set up with respect to that order.

But any given order system lasts only as long as it does, and anyway all ordered things are susceptible to variables that can introduce various ratios of randomness into them.

There are some systems that do not exhibit predictable order at all. These seem totally random in their workings, which produce random side-effects.

In such systems, beginnings are not predictable. So, subsequent effects that transpire from them are also random which means that they are not easily predictable if, at all.

263

A familiar example of a random system is the "mental" part of the human mind that comprises the "seat" of what is referred to as "thinking," the processes of which seem to gather together random data and information the sum of which then tends to be applied to some given end or another – and, as it might be observed, for the better or the worse.

Whatever emerges from the thinking "mental" part of the human mind can be referred as made in the mind, or as "mind-made."

In occult and transcendental philosophies, the basic concept of mind-made is accompanied by several metaphysical connotations that generally refer to higher ranks of "Mind" more or less having cosmic dimensions, and which induce and preserve order therein.

With respect to this, most dictionaries define "Mind" as: "a conscious substratum or factor in the universe."

264

In the human sense, however, MIND has at least three basic definitions that are interactive:

1) the organized conscious and unconscious adaptive activity of an organism;
2) the element or complex of elements in an individual that feels, perceives, thinks, wills, and, especially, reasons;
3) intellectual ability.

These definitions could be read in such a way as to think of the mind as having some kind of order among the whole of the elements pointed up.

However, the processes identified as "feels, perceives, thinks, wills, and, especially, reasons" often demonstrate high susceptibility to variables that can introduce various ratios of randomness into them.

Although not stated in the definitions, the "will" element implies that an individual mind functions so as to begin and output activities that will, via some kind of "time" or timing, fulfill a result, goal, or end point.

Some dozen or so decades ago, various efforts were undertaken on behalf of discovering the intrinsic nature of the human WILL.

The overall result was that the actual intrinsic nature remained ambiguous. But it was ascertained that WILL was some kind of innate principle involved with the dynamics of desire, wish, disposition, inclination, appetite, passion, choice, and determination.

265

What these discussions suggest is that from the human mind there emanate highly random mind-made activities which, depending on the will-dynamics involved, result in strings of impacts of various kind, impacts that are going to happen.

Since it is understood that a rather full part of wisdom consists of realizing and predicting what will happen, it appears that wisdom-making is not only involved with foreseeing WHEN natural events that might come about, but also with what might come about because of mind-made activities, and WHEN.

Chapter Thirty-Nine

WHEN-NESS RATIOS AND THE ODDS

266

WITH REFERENCE to wisdom and wisdom-making, the function of the foregoing discussions has been to make it possible to introduce and elaborate on certain distinctions between:

1) the WHEN-NESS of things that have observable sequences of order that are easily deduced and foreseeable: and
2) the WHEN-NESS of things that have random sequences that are not easily deduced or foreseeable.

Perhaps the first item that might be emphasized has to do with the when-ness RATIO between (1) things that function within some kind of easily predictable sequencing; and (2) the when-ness of things that function within some kind not easily predictable random sequencing.

What the numerical ratio actually consists of has not been well identified and established. But if ALL things are considered, the ratio is at least 50-50. If something like this is the case, humanity exists in an overall environment that is approximately composed of 50 percent ordered and 50 percent random WHEN-NESSES.

267

But then there are the ODDS to consider.

The term ODDS has four definitions that are meaningful in

the contexts of this book:

1) Amount by which one thing exceeds or falls short of another.
2) The probability that one thing is so or will happen rather than another.
3) The RATIO of probability that one thing is so or will happen rather than another.
4) Degree of unlikeness or likeness [obsolete definition].

One factor about wisdom is clearly understood everywhere: whatever it consists of, it had to transcend the odds.

268

In keeping with the teachings of the ancient but still venerable sage, Lao-tsu, all things once started up into activity will eventually have their ultimate outcomes, and between their startups and their ultimate outcomes they will also shed cascading strings of effect-events – and THAT is the Way of the Tao of all Things.

In case one might think that the venerable Lao-tsu is passé, or was talking through his hat, please note that advances in modern and post-modern physics are more or less completely in accord with him.

To get a better grip on this, consider, for example, the differences in startups and outcomes between generative and degenerative activity discussed earlier.

269

Alas! There are certain problems involved if one seeks to consider the Way of All Things – something all wisdom-makers must attempt.

Taking this briefly from an ostensible bigger-picture of the full spectrum of all human activities, it seems clear enough that all of us are born into and expire out of a vast planet-wide environment of generative and degenerative causes and effects that collectively emanate from, of all things, the "mental" part of the fastest computer in existence.

The collective sum of the "mental" parts is as extensive as human populations are at any given time, complicated by the fact that the "mental" parts are innately equipped with memory potentials that can, in one way or another, "remember" the activities of past "mental" parts.

Furthermore, it cannot be said with any certainty that all "mental" parts, past and present, were or are playing with a full deck of cards that might permit optimization of, dare it be said, human survival overall.

Additionally, the start-ups of human activities are entirely difficult to perceive, and so, on average, they become recognizable only in the light (or gloom) of their outcomes.

Finally, there is a certain aspect of the "mental" parts of the fastest computers in existence, an aspect that one hardly dares to suggest or mention.

At least some of them don't seem to have an active capacity to recognize in advance the outcomes of their own mind-made activities. So, it might be thought that surmounting the many odds with respect to saving themselves from themselves could be much in question.

PART EIGHT

INNATE TRANSCENDING CAPACITIES OF THE WISDOM CATEGORY

Chapter Forty

"TIME" TRANSCENDING

270

IT SEEMS APPARENT that what we refer to as wisdom, as a thing-in-itself, is actually produced via various kinds of processes that work together so as to bring about conscious realization of what is going to happen and when it will.

In this sense, wisdom can be divided into two aspects:

1) Identifying or becoming consciously cognizant of what is going to happen when; and
2) Consciously figuring out what do to about it. This is all well and good if it works out.

But there is also a third aspect. This involves sensing something that is going to happen in the absence of any consciously perceived reasons for it.

271

After the existence of the subconscious was identified during the recent modern period, this kind of sensing was simply attributed to it and the matter was let go at that. But this attribution left a number of questions outstanding.

For example: (1) how, and by what processes, can the subconscious sense something that is not being consciously perceived? And (2); how, and by what processes, does the subconscious manage to punch the substance of what IT is sensing into conscious awareness that otherwise has not achieved its OWN awareness of what is involved?

Concerning the second question, it is somewhat understood

that the subconscious and the autonomic systems it contains simply override the parameters of the conscious awareness systems, or, as it might otherwise be put, temporarily transcends them.

This aspect has been quite well researched under the heading of "autonomic reflexes," which, for example, can prompt one's physical body to non-consciously jump out of the way of danger BEFORE sensing anything at all.

This still leaves open why and how the subconscious autonomic systems can sense, identify, and give timing meaning to what they are sensing beneath conscious awareness of whatever is involved. After all, any subconscious sensing of danger before it happens constitutes some sort of "time" transcending.

272

It is worthwhile discussing some intimate details that might be incorporated into the proverbial sensing of danger. One reason for focusing on this is that it is widely accepted as existing – whereas many other types of sensing akin to it are not.

The subconscious sensing of danger before it happens implies that the autonomic systems involved are depending on various kinds of receptors that are providing data and information available to them, but which, for numerous reasons, are not being forwarded into conscious awareness of them.

A further implication is that the autonomic systems seem to possess ways and means of determining this or that meaning, and then to take action that overrides conscious awareness – as, for example, placing the sense of danger into consciousness awareness that didn't have such awareness just before.

One familiar way of describing this is that the subconscious systems have computed something that conscious awareness was not computing.

273

While the concept of COMPUTATION SYSTEM is commonly thought of as involving only mathematical values, the earliest basic definition is given as "a system that determines by reckoning."

The primary definition of RECKON is given as "to determine by reference to a fixed basis," or, as it might also be said, to determine by reference to a fixed program.

In literature relevant to designing artificial intelligent systems, self-regulating processes (such as those comprising the human autonomic nervous system, for example) compute or reckon from fixed bases or programs that are innate within them.

274

AFTER the existence of the self-regulating autonomic nervous systems were actually discovered, which was not too long ago, it was generally assumed that they did not "think" as such but were merely stimulus-response mechanisms.

This appears to be why the term AUTONOMIC was bestowed on them, for that term refers to "largely or wholly involuntary; acting or done spontaneously; having a self-acting or self-regulating mechanism."

(The term INVOLUNTARY, by the way, refers to: "Not subject to control of the conscious will; done contrary to or without choice; not determined by reflective choice.")

Although this makes intellectual sense, there are some hidden difficulties in it – if one merely considers the many examples of sensing danger ahead of time – which is to say, BEFORE whatever is involved can be recognized and determined by reflective, conscious choice that is usually attributed only to the conscious "mental" part of the fastest computer.

275

One full part of the foregoing situation seems to hinge on the central definitions of THINK, to wit: "to determine by pondering a matter over; to determine by reflecting on something; to determine by reflecting on what to do next."

These definitions might as well have included "to determine by pondering and reflecting on what WILL happen next or later, or, on what HAS happened before."

DETERMINE is of course principally defined as: "to settle or decide by choice among alternatives or possibilities.'

Although the concept of PROCESS (say, data and information) is not included in these standard definitions, as a noun, it is nonetheless defined as: "a natural phenomenon marked by changes leading to a particular end result."

As an adjective, it is defined as: "treated or made by special process involving synthesis or artificial modification."

To conceptualize this, it can seem that PROCESS-THINK-DETERMINE are somehow at least partially interrelated and interdependent, if only in that all three lead to this or that end result.

But this clearly implies that the three have beginning points also, such points apparently being determined or reckoned by reference to a fixed basis.

276

DANGER is defined, rather simply, as "exposure or liability to injury, pain, or loss." For some opaque reason, this definition does not incorporate the contexts of destruction or death. Even so, synonyms or aspects of danger, are given as:

DANGEROUS – applies to something that may cause harm or loss unless dealt with carefully.
HAZARDOUS – implies great and continuing risk of harm, or failure and small chance of avoiding disaster.
PRECARIOUS – suggests both insecurity and uncertainty.
RISKY – often applies to a known and accepted danger.

277

These definitions either directly or indirectly suggest that the PROCESS-THINK-DETERMINE thing should be quite intimately involved with respect to danger, etc.

But something of this depends on whether the sources of danger can directly be identified and perceived by conscious awareness.

When such identification and perception depend mostly or completely on the inputs of the five physical senses, and thus can be easily perceived, there is a fair and square chance that some careful handling or avoidance of what is involved can occur.

However, while DANGER might be a thing in itself, as it is often thought to be, any perception of it results from processes that are themselves first pre-conscious.

As mentioned earlier, it is now quite well understood that anything and everything that emerges AS perception into the neo-cortex of the brain is preceded by numerous kinds of pre-conscious processes that busy themselves with "receiving" millions of data bits that are then analyzed, processed, assembled, packaged, and synthesized first into pre-conscious perception.

It is only then that a pre-conscious perception might or might not emerge into the neo-cortex where, it is thought, all conscious perception takes place.

So, there are two kinds of perception of danger – pre-conscious ones, and conscious ones.

278

Furthermore, when all of the elements that comprise danger might be examined, there is always some kind of TIMING FACTOR involved. Any sense or perception of danger at least implies that one is still alive in the Now in order to sense or perceive it – as Teddy Roosevelt put it, "in time."

This "in time," of course refers to "before it happens." Recognition of "before it happens" always incorporates some kind of "time" transcending.

Since the sensing and perceiving of danger is such an important aspect regarding all things small to large, the foregoing might find some small place in a general educational course entitled DANGER 101. Ever head of such a thing? So, we plod on in the absence of such.

279

There are many recorded of this kind of thing by those who lived to tell about it. As many record, "I sensed danger," and "it's too bad I didn't heed it," or "it's too bad I didn't have the wisdom to heed it." Some say that "something in me sensed danger that I didn't consciously recognize."

This latter observation is probably more to the point, because it implies that there is "something in me" beneath conscious recognition that incorporates the required "time" transcending capacity in order to recognize what's going to happen at some WHEN point ahead whether near or far.

280

As has been mentioned earlier, during the last four decades or so a great deal has been learned about senses and perceptions.

To repeat, basically speaking, a SENSE or a PERCEPTION cannot take place unless and until millions of incoming data bits are, via pre-conscious processes, sorted, analyzed, and synthesized so as to result in the given end products we refer to as a sense or a perception.

In sensing danger before it happens, the "before it happens" aspect has to include a "time" transcending function or potential.

It is not unreasonable to think that such functions and potentials are fundamentally innate in our species – on the grounds that they seem universal enough in all cultures, and, as well, evidence of them figures back into ancient and even archaic epochs.

Although such time transcending potentials might not be accessible within the contexts of this or that intellectual configuration (i.e., reality box), they are clearly displayed via a sense of danger before it becomes perceptually evident.

They also display themselves in instances of wisdom-making in which sensing what is going to happen plays a significant role, and which role Teddy Roosevelt indicated as comprising "Nine- tenths of wisdom . . ."

Chapter Forty-One

EXTRAPOLATE VERSUS TRANSCEND

281

DURING THE MODERN PERIOD, it was somehow established that the human mind could not ACTUALLY transcend time, but that it could, by various kinds of intellectually designed computational systems, "predict" what might happen ahead.

For the most part, such computational systems were basically set up so as "to determine by reference to a fixed basis."

This "fixed basis" sometimes included events that had happened in the past, but more usually were only based on what was happening in the NOW.

282

These computational systems can be utilized to predict only in the case where the phenomena being considered have a recognized self-repeating order of timing, and whose random variables are minimal. Otherwise, what might happen ahead can only be extrapolated, rather than predicted.

EXTRAPOLATE is principally defined as: "to project, extend, or expand known data or experience into an area not known or experienced so as to arrive at a usually conjectural knowledge of the unknown area by inferences based on an assumed continuity, correspondence, or other parallelism between it and what is known." Whee! Did you get it? If not, the key words are "conjectural" and "assumed."

In the light of this, it can be thought if the human mind

cannot actually transcend time, then it can only work within conjectural extrapolations of what might happen ahead.

283

Now, it can be admitted, based on copious evidence for it, that the human mind might not actually transcend time. But what about other aspects or parts of the human organism – for instance, the subconscious autonomic systems, or, in the last consideration, human consciousness itself?

Is one to think, for example, that the subconscious sensing of danger is merely extrapolated, which is to say, conjectured from all possibilities available to extrapolation?

Well, CONJECTURE is defined as: "inference from defective or assumptive evidence." The workings and processes of the proverbial sense of danger seem more precise than that, and many have been grateful thereby.

Chapter Forty-Two

IS TIME TRANSCENDING INNATE IN HUMAN CONSCIOUSNESS?

284

IF it can be thought that the proverbial sense of danger does not just simply conjecture the danger as a possibility, but rather must actually transcend time in order to, say, determine and spot the danger ahead, then human consciousness overall is somehow equipped with at least one innate kind of time transcending capacity.

This has direct application to wisdom-making overall, for it seems unlikely that wisdom can be achieved, except via some unlikely chance, if it is based merely on conjecturing and extrapolating.

In this sense, the time-transcending dynamic of wisdom is more in keeping with the time-transcending dynamic of the sense of danger, both dynamics seemingly having to do to with innate human consciousness itself rather than with the somewhat wobbly constituents of this or that conscious mind.

285

One of the basic problems within all of this has to do with the term TRANSCEND and the many psychological and philosophical confusions that have accumulated around it.

The prefix TRANS- refers to "across, beyond, through, so as to change."

Our English term TRANSCEND is taken from the Latin TRANS

+ SCANDERE, meaning "to climb above."

In English, TRANSCEND simply means "to rise above or go beyond the limits of," and in reading this definition, dictionaries indicate that SCAN should also be consulted.

Our English SCAN (also taken from the Latin SCANDERE) is defined in a number of ways, among which are "to make a sweeping search of," and also "to direct a succession of radar beams over in searching for a target."

Basically speaking, when using an elevator, one is transcending the stairs that would otherwise need to be climbed or descended. If one uses a skywalk over a busy highway, one is transcending the traffic below.

286

But the term "transcend" is seldom utilized in connection with these simple transcendings, largely, perhaps, because the term has OTHER definitions – such as "to be prior to, above, and beyond the universe or, especially, material existence."

This particular definition leads into those of TRANSCENDENT, i.e., "exceeding or surpassing usual limits; extending or lying beyond the limits of ordinary experience; transcending the universe of material existence."

It is at this point, in modern times anyway, that committed materialists, their sciences and philosophies, parted company with the term TRANSCEND – and, as well, relegated anything smelling of the transcendental to "superstition," including the notion that time can be transcended by some aspect or function innate in human consciousness.

287

Even so, there exists (prior to modern times) a long history of accumulated evidence that more than suggests that somewhere in human consciousness overall are innate factors that transcend and surpass at least the limits of the five physical senses, the limits of conscious perception, the limits of this or that conscious mind, and even the limits of this or that kind of conscious knowledge packages.

There is also copious evidence that transcending, and

surpassing have benefited almost all human activities, not only when it comes to surviving danger, but also to creativeness, inventiveness, innovation, problem solving, and, of all things, wisdom-making and planning and initiating activities for pro-survival in times ahead in the face of all the odds against it.

Chapter Forty-Three

INNATE TRANSCENDING "VEHICLES" IN HUMAN CONSCIOUSNESS

288

AS MENTIONED EARLIER, the definitions of (to) THINK hinge on words such as reflect, ponder, and determine. Synonyms are given as cogitate, reason, speculate, deliberate, intend, and plan.
These are further extended by the terms conceive, imagine, fancy, realize, and envision.

For some obscure reason, the concept of mentally processing, assembling, organizing, and aligning data and information is not included in the definitions, and neither is the concept of mentally MAKING some kind of order out of what one experiences and learns.

These and other concepts might come to light if there existed an educational course entitled THINKING 101, and such a course might aid in better optimization of human thinking overall.

As it is, however, although the existence of thinking capacities in our species are everywhere accepted as innate, individuals having such capacities are more or less left to then-own ways and means and to what to do with them.

289

In the contexts of our human species, the concepts of TO MAKE and MAKING are enormously significant, so much so that it could even be thought they outrank intelligence. Indeed, back when it was being decided what to name our species, some opined that it should be identified as HOMO FABRICANS, i.e., Man who fabricates things.

This refers to a HOMO species that creates, invents, innovates, constructs, manufactures, and makes with reference to just about everything – and which capacities are so abundantly existing that they by far out-strip all other known animate organisms and the species to which they belong.

The term MAKE is so significant as to have at least some twenty-seven definitions in smaller concise dictionaries, and ninety-nine plus in the authoritative Oxford English Dictionary.

However, it is necessary to review only a few definitions of MAKE:

"To cause to happen or be experienced by someone;
"To cause to exist, happen, or occur;
"To cause to be or become;
"To compute or estimate to be;
"To bring into being by forming, shaping, or altering matter or materials [and, as might be mentioned, of ideas and understandings as well];
"To set in order;
"To frame or formulate in the mind;
"To fit, intend, or destine by or as if creating."

(Please note that the definitions are mutually interdependent and interactive. So they have not been numbered, which might falsely suggest some kind of precedence among them.)

One reason for laboring through all of this is that if some daring soul were to attempt to make a larger understanding of wisdom and wisdom-making, the above definitions would somehow have to be incorporated into it.

290

Returning now to discussions of THINK, it can be observed that its relevant definitions of pondering, reflecting, and determining are obviously considered as applying to conscious thinking in the consciously awake state of the mind. The reason for making this observation is that the principle definition of "think" is given as "to have or form in the mind" within which what is being thought about is consciously accessible.

Well, the mind has other states – for example, the sleep state during which it is not awake, and other attenuated states of awake-ness, and which can include total unconsciousness.

Something of course depends on how the mind is being defined, i.e., perhaps so as to include the subconscious and its various aspects. But even so, the activities of pondering, reflecting, determining, and, especially, of reasoning are usually attributed to the cognitive functions of the awake mind.

Although these considerations might seem a little wobbly, it is the case that no one expects or anticipates that the awake mind thinks unless it is awake to do so.

And very few think that the awake mind can be transcended by something that transcends the awake mind's thinking processes and boundaries – especially its "rational" logic--reasoning processes that have a long history of being attributed entirely to the awake conscious mind.

Anything that does so has been considered (certainly in our late, great rational modern times at least) as irrational and illogical.

291

The concept of "intuitive thinking" does exist. But if the definitions of INTUITION are studied and adhered to, it seems to be a mere intellectualism set up by those who have not experienced an example of it.

The fundamental definition of INTUITION is given as: "the power or faculty of attaining to direct knowledge or cognition without rational thought or inference."

The "without thought" part is clearly meant to directly state that an intuitive event is not a result of "thinking," at least if the definitions of that term are acknowledged and adhered to.

The same can be said of the "direct cognition" part that establishes that such cognition has NOT been preceded by any recognizable pondering, reflective, determining, or reasoning processes of the awake mind that establish what thinking consists of per se.

What might be the case is that an intuition might occur when the thinking processes self-realize, as it were, that their pondering, reflecting, and reasoning are NOT ENOUGH.

Indeed, pondering, reflecting, and reasoning processes can take place only with respect to what is already known, rationalized, and incorporated into them. What is not already known cannot be rationalized and worked into such processes.

So, when "direct knowledge and cognition" without thinking takes place, the former should be acknowledged as transcending the latter.

292

One aspect of intuition that doesn't seem very well noted or studied involves the fact that intuition occurs all of the time, albeit along a scale ranging from small to big. Small-time intuition is barely recognized as such, even by those experiencing it, whereas big-time intuitions can achieve renown and glamour.

If intuitions did not occur all of the time, then specimens of our species would be more or less trapped within the limited configurations of their thinking, which is to say, trapped within the limits of what they know, or think they do.

In any event, more pro-survival wisdom-making has arisen from "direct knowledge or cognitions" ascribed to intuitions than from limited configurations of conscious thinking.

293

One outstanding question of all has to do with the matter of how intuitions proceed into their manifestations. For clarity, it can reasonably be accepted that intuition emerges from within deeply unknown depths of human consciousness itself. But there still remains the question of the processes via which the intuition achieves cognitive awareness.

To scratch the surface of this, it is first necessary to enter into a bigger picture of our species, and then to consider whether innate human consciousness per se is hell bent on achieving its own ultimate destruction versus its pro-survival.

It is quite apparent that MIND-THINKING is innate in our species, and that via that capacity specimens of our species can make into existence anything they want.

Yet, as our recorded history demonstrates, such mind-thinking obviously has something of a rather high failure rate regarding ultimate pro-survival.

294

In order to scratch a little deeper, one might consider whether innate human consciousness per se can be thought of as a naturally intelligent system or if it is an entirely non-intelligent random affair.

If the latter were the case, then outcomes would consist of meltdowns in direct ratio to the randomness involved. In other words, our species and individual specimens would consist of something like self-disintegrating blobs with but minimal capacity to procreate, if at all.

Most dictionaries indicate that a "system" consists of component parts that interact with one another, and let it go at that.

However, advances relevant to designing artificial intelligence have gone a couple of steps further by establishing that through the interactions of the parts and their relationships to this or that environment, the components may give rise to "the emergence, or genesis, of "systemic behaviors that transcend" those of the individual components.

EMERGENCE also takes place not only with respect to environments, but also to instability arising from among systemic components.

These instabilities would result in wild swings toward precarious tendencies, which, if not corrected, would lead to ultimate failure and crashing of the system.

In terms of innovating artificial intelligent systems, emergent "suppression of instability" is a central concern relevant to designing them, and this should be the case with respect to natural intelligent systems as well.

295

If the gist of the above is superimposed onto natural intelligent systems (such as our own intelligent species system represents), then long ago there must have emerged in them self- correcting capacities to deal with wild instabilities that would otherwise lead to ultimate systemic failure.

Furthermore, such capacities would have had to acquire an innate status, so as to be forwarded into subsequent generations of the system. Otherwise, each subsequent generation would be a self-perpetuating blob of instabilities.

In other words, overall innate human consciousness per se MUST possess somewhere within it equally innate capacities to deal with, correct, and mitigate its own instability potentials.

To proceed with this particular discussion about instabilities, a slight digression is first required.

296

When a reasonably impressive instance of intuition occurs, there is a strong tendency to focus on the information content delivered rather than on the mechanisms that have facilitated the information delivery.

For clarity, MECHANISM refers to "a process or technique for achieving a result." However, INTUITION is defined as "the power or faculty of attaining direct knowledge or cognition without rational thought or inference."

This definition implies a two-step formula consisting of (1) from source directly to (2) cognition, without any mechanisms being involved between (1) and (2).

However, the definition of INTUITION includes "the power or faculty of attaining to."

FACULTY has several definitions, the first and most principal of which is given as: "a natural ability, power, or capacity."

Three principal definitions of NATURAL are given as: (1) an inherent sense or function; (2) characterized by qualities held to be part of the nature of man; and (3) free from artificiality, affectation, or constraint.

297

If all of the above definitions are considered together as parts of the whole they represent, then the definition for INTUITION ought to be slightly amended: "the natural power or natural faculty for achieving a result of direct knowledge or cognition that transcends constraints of rational thought or inference."

298

It is at least somewhat illogical to suppose that a natural (hence innate) faculty involving natural ability, power, or capacity can function in the absence of equally innate fundamental mechanisms via which they emerge as such and incorporate the characteristics they do.

EMERGE is defined as "to become manifest; to arise from an obscure or inferior condition."

However, EMERGENT EVOLUTION is defined as: "Evolution characterized by the appearance at different levels of wholly new and unpredictable characters or qualities through rearrangement of preexisting entities."

ENTITY is defined as "independent, separate, or self-contained existence," and "something that has separate and distinct existence and objective or conceptual reality."

299

If intuition transcends the constraints of rational thought and inference, then it could be thought of as having independent, separate, or self-contained existence AND as having distinct existence as objective and conceptual reality that EMERGE into awareness – if and when they do, and even if such awareness is unprepared for the emergence.

It is easily recognized that emergent intuition (like emergent wisdom) conveys information that involves objective and conceptual realities to the degree that it re-conceptualizes prior conceptual ones.

300

Returning now to the consideration of systemic instabilities, any natural life intelligent systems probably won't survive too well or too long unless mechanisms internal to them are self-induced and evolved so as to correct and even protect against instabilities per se.

Furthermore, unless such mechanisms are not incorporated into the prevailing innateness of such systems, then they probably won't be forwarded into their subsequent generations.

301

If this might seem somehow familiar, it is probably because these discussions have moved into an approximate vicinity of an important and ever on-going situational problem that has been known, considered, and acted upon for several millennia.

In recent times, it situation has been referred to as involving the FAIL-SAFE problem, i.e., the designing and setting up of measures "incorporating some feature for automatically safeguarding against or counteracting the effect of an anticipated possible source of failure."

FAILURE is rather simply designated as: "omission of occurrence or performance."

302

It might be that innovators and designers of artificial intelligence are more intimately involved with the fail-safe scenario than are many specimens of our species possessing natural intelligence.

The reason is that fail-safe measures need to be designed into artificial intelligent machines, at least into advanced and more elegant kinds of them such as "intelligent" robots.

If not, such machines could not correct for their own instabilities that might ultimately lead to their "omission of occurrence and performance."

Of course, such artificial intelligent machines cannot so far reproduce themselves per se. But their circuitry can be copied and manufactured – and that possibility has led to many worrisome science fiction scenarios in which highly advanced intelligent robots learn to copy their circuitry and end up ruling the world.

303

Meanwhile, back at the ranch of human endeavors, if one takes an interest in finding out what wisdom consists of, the definitions of failure and fail-safe constitute some full part of its overall workings.

Within the human perspective, however, there are no general educational courses that might be entitled FAILURE 101 and FAIL-SAFE 101. And so individual specimens have to do the best they can on their own initiative.

304

Although not often recognized as such, one function of intuition tends to become cognizable if we but consider the proverbial sensing of danger ahead of time, and which is often attributed to intuition.

The apparent purpose behind the DELIVERING of the sensing of danger into awareness that has not itself managed to recognize the danger, more than suggests that some kind "corrections" are necessary, corrections that transcend the limits of rational thought and inference.

In other words, a fail-safe something or other has somewhere in human consciousness overall been activated and conveyed.

305

If one studies how wisdom and intuition are generally viewed, they are often considered to be things in themselves, especially if judged only by their products.

But this might not actually be the case. What is clear enough about them is that their elements emerge, if they can, into cognitive consciousness. So it is taken for granted that they have done so from some particular source, sometimes thought to be subconscious, but sometimes thought to be external to a given individual consciousness – and which is a possibility if, say, interactive telepathy among entities is considered.

However, the term EMERGE is associated with the concept of EMERGENT EVOLUTION, the definition of which has already been discussed, but is repeated here: "Evolution characterized by the appearance at different levels (say, of innate consciousness) of wholly new and unpredictable characters or QUALITIES through a rearrangement of preexisting entities."

306

With respect to wisdom, which is undeniably supported by various kinds of intuition, at least one interpretation of the above definition is possible and worth examining.

It can certainly be thought that among all its inherent "equipment" innate human consciousness has innate ways and means of transferring and delivering information among and throughout its "different levels," and which, all things considered, seem to be quite numerous.

Even so, something of this has to do with what kinds information need to be delivered or conveyed to which level, including the "level" of awake cognitive awareness.

Such delivery or conveyance systems might be innately fixed within the whole of innate consciousness.

But the innate consciousness "package" actually exists, lives, and evolves in the contexts of information environments within which information meanings shift and change about in wild profusion – albeit apparently somewhat in keeping with information contexts relevant to this or that historical epoch or "times."

307

One implication of this is that information that served as a basis for intuition and wisdom in the past might not automatically serve as a basis for, say, any given present or future and which past bases must therefore be transcended by some function innate in human consciousness.

In other words, although innate human consciousness must have innate faculties that decode and recognize meanings of information per se, such faculties would ultimately prove inefficient unless they were accompanied by emergent characteristics capable of evolving more or less in keeping with evolving information.

In similar fashion, the intuition category and the wisdom category that exist somewhere innate in human consciousness must also have emergent qualities.

The innate basis of this must assuredly consist of processes that permit rearrangement and remixing of preexisting information entities, but the whole of which, to be efficient, must evolve in keeping with new information entities.

308

After all of the above has been said, there still remains the issue of the ways and means via which information that transcends rational thought and inference might be conveyed, carried, and transferred so as to converge as "direct cognition."

CONVEY is principally defined as "to bear from one place to another; to transport; to carry; to transfer."

These definitions imply the existence of some sort of VEHICLE that carries or conveys whatever.

309

In ancient India and elsewhere in the Far East, numerous metaphysical psychologies and philosophies utilized terms equivalent to our understanding of "vehicle" that carried, transferred, and even TRANSFORMED information into meanings appropriate to various levels of total human consciousness.

The concept of vehicle was also applied to the many different levels of Mind, the least and most insignificant aspect of which was the awake conscious mind that worked only within the parameters of its own rationalizing "illusions."

In utilizing the concept of vehicle this way, the Eastern ancients became metaphorically enabled to designate various kinds of them with a specialized or unique entity-like status having "separate and distinct existence and objective and conceptual reality."

This seems to imply that the Eastern ancients could identify objective and conceptual realities with a vehicular Way that carried each of them in the particular way they did.

This is at least somewhat commensurate with current scientific understanding that different kinds of information are carried and transferred in ways specific to their functioning – and that if the vehicular ways get jumbled then ambiguous, meaningless "noise" is all that results.

310

TRANSCEND is defined as: "to rise or go beyond the limits of; exceed; surpass; to be prior to, beyond and above the universe of material existence."

These definitions reflect active contexts that are extremely old within our species, and which can be identified as innately existing even in archaic periods, and probably even in the fogs of the primordial past.

Furthermore, these contexts have survived all mind-made instabilities in our species and cataclysms thought to have happened in the distant past. The basic reason for this surviving is simply that such contexts are born anew in all specimens of our species no matter where.

It might even be considered, theoretically at least, that to transcend might be the first survival goal of our species, which clearly has something to do with transcending the many odds against surviving.

311

Since these contexts are so very ancient, it clearly appears that vehicles for transcending have become innate in human consciousness, and that evolutionary emergence of them is fully ongoing within the innate levels of our emergent evolution.

If something like this is the case, then various transcending vehicles ought to have been consciously recognized and linguistically categorized very long ago. Indeed, such linguistic categorizing can be seen to exist in all languages including English that, by comparison to antiquity of ALL languages, is still a very young one.

312

In English there are dozens of linguistic categorizations that are assigned and refer to this or that kind or type of transcending vehicle as consisting of a separate and distinct conceptual reality.

On the surface of this, the process of assigning linguistic name terms to a conceptual reality seems sensible enough, since doing so thereafter permits easy and discrete reference to and discussion of whatever is involved. So it is this process that enables language to be used in some coherent way, even if only approximately so.

313

But there are some subtle drawbacks to this process that are seldom recognized as such. One of these has to do with the widespread tendency to think that once a term has been assigned to something, then what has been named is a thing-in-itself. This tendency works well enough with physical things that can, with a modicum of conscious mental ease, be perceived and accounted for via the five physical senses. After all, an apple is a thing in itself, and in any language.

But this thing-in-itself tendency doesn't work too well in the case conceptual realities that have achieved the status of being consciously recognized as such and have been assigned a terminological name. The central problem here has two parts, both of which might not be easy to grasp. Don't worry too much about this, for such matters might clear up via discussions yet ahead.

First, once a conceptual reality has been named, there is a general tendency to think that the NAME itself concretely objectifies what has been named as a thing-in-itself in the same way that naming physical things does.

Second, there is a general tendency to think that the NAME itself can evoke, invoke, and provides what might be called conscious cognitive mental access INTO the conceptual realities that have been named as things-in-themselves. This MAY be workable depending on what is involved, but it tends to be unworkable if conceptual realities are NOT discrete things-in-themselves.

314

In the contexts of this book for example, somewhere in the distant past of our species it appears that certain behavioral phenomena of humans themselves were conceptually recognized as beneficial with respect to building mechanisms for survival in the present and into the future.

Such "recognition" obviously belongs among what we today collectively refer to as "conceptual realities." We have no way of knowing what names in which language were established for such past conceptual recognition(s), or even if names were established at all.

Jumping ahead in time, such conceptual recognitions obviously became associated with experience and then learning about what was beneficial or not.

At some further point ahead, say in ancient Egypt, China, India, and presumably elsewhere, documented evidence exists indicating that such pro-survival learning became associated with, for example, sagacity which achieved the status of both a conceptual reality and a conceptual entity having its own ways of activity.

315

In our present times, SAGACIOUS is defined, in English, as what results from qualities "of keen and farsighted penetration, discernment, and judgment," and which qualities, as already suggested, obviously act as vehicles that support and help produce sagacity.

Now, focusing on the term-name SAGACIOUS, if considered as a thing-in-itself, might not, and probably won't, evoke or invoke conscious mental connection to the vehicular qualities enumerated in its English definition. Go ahead. Try it.

There is one definition of the term that might be a little more efficient in this respect, but which, for opaque reasons, is given as obsolete: i.e., "keen in sense perception." Something here of course depends on what "sense perception(s)" are thought to be in this or that reality box.

Since this particular definition is given as obsolete, it obviously conceptually existed before the theory of the "five physical senses only" came into existence during the latter part of the famous Age of Reason and Enlightenment.

316

It is easy enough to comprehend that the conceptual realities of sagacity have been incorporated into our present concept of wisdom, that concept itself having taken on its own status as a conceptual reality.

To refresh, our English definitions of WISDOM are briefly given, in the following order, as:

1) Accumulated philosophical or scientific learning and knowledge;
2) Ability to discern inner qualities and relationships insight;
3) Good sense and judgment;
4) A wise attitude or course of action.

Although one might wonder about the actual authenticity of the first definition, these four definitions serve as well as they might or might not. Please note, however, that the conceptual reality of sagacity seems not to be incorporated into them.

317

There is a further wonderment behind the foregoing definitions.

If one examines the etymological background of the word WISDOM, it will be discovered that it was apparently evolved from the proto-English word WISSIAN that is translated as: "To make known, give information of, indicate; especially to show or point out (the way)."

These older proto-English definitions do not seem to be too much cognitively incorporated into, or even implied by, the later concepts of wisdom. But they are directly implicit in the workings of what we refer to as INTUITION.

It can now to noted that the definitions of the proto-English WISSIAN describe not what intuition IS, but what it actually DOES, in that it makes known, gives information of, indicates, and, especially shows out the way. There is, after all, a difference between what something is and what it does.

Although not included in definitions of WISDOM, this latter aspect is fully expected of it –for if wisdom, like sagacity, cannot point out the way then it is relatively useless.

318

As discussed earlier, intuition achieved the status of being recognized as a conceptual reality and did so as early as ancient Roman times. But, as already mentioned, dozens upon dozens of other transcending vehicles also achieved the status of conceptual reality, and all were assigned entity-like terms and names so as to establish nomenclature frames of reference for them.

During the twentieth century, all such terms and the phenomena they referred to were classified into what was assumed to be the "paranormal" category. This is a designation so entirely familiar and used that one might think it has been with us for a very long time.

However, it must be noted up that the term PARANORMAL is of such recent vintage that it had not yet been inducted into the authoritative Oxford Dictionary of the English Language as of its 1971 edition.

319

Even so, the presumed essence of its meanings has been established here and there, and these presumptions have yielded equally presumptive definitions for it.

The etymology of the term is fundamentally based on the concept of the psychological "abnormal." During the 1920s and the 1930s, this term was generally defined and applied as "deviating from the norm or average."

This definition is appropriate to numerous things, but when it is applied to human psychological behavior it translates into a stigma. After all, most want to be considered as interactively normal, and so anything that might suggest otherwise is to be feared and hidden away from the prying eyes of the normal.

320

The stigma of being abnormal proved to have some rather tough and socially objectionable edges to it. These were somewhat smoothed over and softened by the introduction of the term PARANORMAL.

In its early usage, it was defined as anything that was "not scientifically explainable," which definition by itself was workable. But almost in the same breath, what was not scientifically explainable was dubbed as superstition that incorporated "an irrational belief or practice resulting from ignorance."

Thus, the paranormal could be stigmatized as irrational whether or not it was based in irrational superstition, irrational intelligence, irrational minds, irrational ignorance, of even in the irrationalities of the completely unknown, and all of which deviate from this or that established norm.

321

If one has the time and persistence to survey the larger whole of the so-called paranormal, it's not too difficult to discover that the worst irrational offender that is "not scientifically explainable" turns out to consist of anything that transcends something else – and/or the activities of transcendence itself.

Yet, as has been discussed, such transcending goes on all of the time – even in the conscious mind, for example, within which contemplation on various things can result in intuitive transcending of former mind-made limits that had been applied to them.

322

At this juncture, this author cannot resist pointing up that wisdom and sagacity are not normally present, and are even absent, within the contexts of whatever can be considered as representative of the normal. One needs only to observe many existing normal status quo conditions to infer as much.

If these absences are applied against scales by which the normal versus the abnormal are measured, then wisdom and sagacity will fall into the abnormal category – and nothing is really to be gained by softening this by depending on the term "paranormal."

323

As has been mentioned earlier, whatever was "not scientifically explainable" in modern scientific contexts was relegated to the rather monumental heap of the irrational.

This trashing included the phenomena of the major offenders, human transcending categories, but also the very WORDS and NAMES used to identify them as conceptual realities.

A short list of such words will be provided ahead. But to segue into that list, it is worthwhile considering a few transcending conceptual realities and their names that no one has ever dared to trash as irrational.

324

AWARENESS. Although there appear to be many different capacities of awareness, they are considered as innately existing in our species, and within the innate folds of consciousness itself.

One difficulty that seems to stand in the way of fully conceptualizing the magnitudes of awareness is that it appears to have many levels, some of which are very "deep." These levels function of their own accord, but nevertheless can emerge into conscious awareness thereby transcending its limits.

Another difficulty is that awareness is usually considered a discrete thing-in-itself. So little more need be said or inquired into it.

But if all known elements of awareness are brought together, it will at least seem that it is MANY things in itself in possession of manifold awareness qualities that serve different functions and purposes in intra-changeable ways.

That awareness cannot be thought of as a discrete thing-in-itself has more or less been confirmed by, of all things, studies in evolving and designing artificial intelligence.

Via these studies, it is increasingly understood that artificial intelligence depends on some kind of "awarenesses" that cannot be discreetly "static" in their separate selves.

Instead, such awarenesses and their differing levels of qualitative perception need to work through a continuing rearrangement of preexistent entities. This suggests that the essential "nature" of awareness is actually a continuously recombinant one.

325

INTELLIGENCE. Like awareness, intelligence is typically thought of as a thing-in-itself, the dimensions of which can be measured via various IQ measuring routines.

It may be that such routines can measure conscious intelligence parameters as these have been formatted usually within the contexts of various environmental and social scenarios.

Even so, it is generally understood (by just about everyone) that conscious intelligence is not all there is to innate intelligence, which is at least suspected as having different levels, some quite "deep," in much the same way that awareness is known to have.

It seems that conscious formats of intelligence do not usually transcend themselves, but that such can be transcended by, as it were, bigger and larger strata of innate intelligence.

For example, conscious intelligence can be transcended by non-conscious forms of it via dreams, contemplations, various intuitions, other transcending vehicles, and even by the simplicities of experiencing and learning.

326

INNATENESS. Debate and argument can take place, via this or that reality box intellectualism, as to what is or is not thought to be innate in our species. But the conceptual reality of The Innate can hardly be thought of as being irrational. Indeed, if parts of The Innate, or the sum functioning of them, were irrational, instabilities would then occur at a great rate to the point where the collective innateness would self-destruct.

Our English term INNATE is taken from the Latin IN + NASCI

meaning "inborn, or to be born with." The most common English versions of this are: "belonging to the inherent essential nature of something; existing in or belonging to an individual from birth; existing in a person's organism from birth; belonging to the original constitution of body and mind".

These four are the only English definitions – implying that the meanings of the definitions are so self-evident that little more needs to be said.

However, the fourth definition might be amended to read: "belonging to the original constitution of body, mind, and the innate consciousness that incorporates them."

At the end of this matter, it is innateness that is indelibly propagated into successive generations of our species. This can only mean that innateness, by procreating itself, can and will transcend all else that might otherwise occur within the vicissitudes of conscious mind-made activities.

327

COMPASSION. There exists copious evidence that the qualities of compassion can be stigmatized as irrational by those in whom its innate essence and elements have not manifested.

But if innate human consciousness per se was totally bereft of its compassion categories, then the odds against its ultimate survival might have won the day long ago.

For clarity, COMPASSION is usually thought of as "having pity." But the term is basically defined as "sympathetic consciousness of others' distress together with a desire to alleviate it."

The "desire to alleviate it" part of compassion's definition suggests some kind of dynamic active measures, while "having pity" is suggestive of non-dynamic passiveness.

SYMPATHETIC is defined as "existing or operating through an affinity, interdependence, or mutual association; not discordant or antagonistic; showing empathy."

EMPATHY is basically defined as "the capacity for participating in another's feelings or ideas."

PARTICIPATE is rather briefly defined as: "to partake of; to share in; to possess something of the nature of a person, thing, or quality."

Now, the concept of participating in, partaking of, and sharing objectively realizable concrete things is very well understood, and indeed, since archaic and ancient times a large part of the human world has actually turned on this concept.

But the terms utilized to expand on the definition of compassion include EMPATHY, "the capacity for participating in another's FEELINGS or IDEAS."

It is the case that one can participate with another's feelings or ideas AFTER they have been objectively expressed, identified, and consciously recognized as such. But this is a conscious, intellectual process, is it not?

It does not at all reflect the original intent behind the emergence of the word "empathy," which is in such widespread use as to think it has been around for a very long time.

The term was actually coined in 1912 and was originally defined as "The power of directly entering into the experience of or the understanding of objects or emotions outside ourselves." It is accepted and established that all intellectual processes, in so far as they are presently understood, take place within ourselves.

So, the original intent of the definition of EMPATHY was to point up the existence of a "power" that directly transcends our internalized, and often limited, intellectual processes, a power that exists somewhere within the innate powers of human consciousness itself.

It is worth mentioning that before the emergence of EMPATHY was seized upon to denote a particular type of conceptual reality, the workings of empathy had been attributed to various transcending kinds of intuition. Indeed, what we now refer to as empathy has, via other linguistic terms, a very long history in our species as a whole.

If all of the terms utilized to denote COMPASSION in its broader sense as a conceptual reality, then the transcending component of the "power" of empathy plays a much larger role than has otherwise been identified.

Passive and therefore inactive compassion of course equates to pity. In its active sense as the desire to alleviate distress, it would more or less have to transcend the elements involved in distress in order to figure out ways and means of alleviating them. After all, alleviating distress cannot too much be achieved by only dealing within the elements of distress. It must somehow be transcended in order to recognize the sources and causes of distress.

Active compassion is therefore the opposite of discordant and antagonistic phenomena that introduce instabilities. And when unitive and empathic active compassion prevails, such phenomena decline, and the processes of pro-survival can get underway again.

If all things are considered, the survival of our species probably owes a great deal to the Way of empathic compassion whose innate categories are somewhere incorporated into its innate procreating consciousness.

328

UNDERSTANDING. Finally, there is the matter of the conceptual reality identified and named UNDERSTANDING, which is taken from the Old English words UNDER + STANDAN that meant "to stand under something."

Twentieth century definitions, however, define that conceptual reality as consisting of: "discernment; insight; the act or result of interpreting; the power of comprehending; specifically, the capacity to apprehend general relations of particulars; the power to make experience intelligible by applying concepts and categories; endowed with understanding." There are three archaic, therefore obsolete, definitions: "knowing; intelligent; sympathetic."

These definitions, including the archaic ones, seem straightforward enough, except for the part given as "endowed with understanding."

ENDOWMENT is basically defined as "natural [i.e., innate] capacity, power, or ability." But "understanding" is commonly thought not to be innate, but to be ACQUIRED by consciously undergoing study, tutoring, instruction, and experience from the scopes of which discernment, comprehending, and interpreting can result.

The inclusion of the term INSIGHT in the definitions is also something of a glitch because it is defined as: "the act of apprehending the inner nature of things or of seeing intuitively; the penetrating power or act of seeing into a situation."

Well, the standard definition of SEEING, or to SEE, is given as "to perceive by the eye," i.e., to perceive by the first of the five physical senses.

If all of the definitions of UNDERSTANDING are considered together, then the implication is that at least two types of it are defined as existing. A type acquired via the physical eye, and a type that apparently involves other processes that transcend the limitations of the physical eye – processes, it might be noted, that were stigmatized as irrational during the twentieth century, even though they were legitimized as existing in standard dictionaries and encyclopedias.

Be that as it may, it is generally understood and broadly accepted that understanding has many levels, many degrees of efficiency, and, as well, many limits demarked by this or that degree of it.

It is also accepted that, say, lesser and limited formats of understanding can be transcended by an emerging greater format, which can eventuate in radical shifts in apprehending, discerning, interpreting, and comprehending.

If ALL of its dictionary definitions are considered together, it appears that what is called "understanding" is perhaps the most mobile and most transcending vehicle within innate human consciousness not only having objective and conceptual realities, but also dictionary and encyclopedic definitions.

329

One reason for dragging through the definitions of awareness, intelligence, innateness, compassion, and understanding is to point up that these qualities are not static within given intellectual limits or given frames of reference, but instead are, from bottom to top, entirely transcending in their essential nature. If they were not, then all of them would be stopped dead within this or that frame of limits.

There is another reason for laboring through the definitions. This has to do with the rather unassailable fact that in their transcending nature, the qualities of awareness, intelligence, innateness, compassion, and understanding are obvious, and even necessary, components of wisdom and wisdom-making.

If such components were static within the contexts of self-limiting, intellectualized frames of reference, then not too much wisdom could be generated from them.

Indeed, it is fully expected that wisdom and wisdom-making MUST transcend all intellectual, mind-made limits that might prevent wisdom from being made.

330

There is yet another point to be made by trudging through the five definitions of categories of awareness, intelligence, innateness, compassion, and understanding.

Although their transcending aspects are tacitly accepted as existing (in dictionaries, anyway), they are seldom openly referred to as such – even though no one really expects, or even wants, those categories to remain in a static condition that ceases to be developable.

This is especially the case with awareness, intelligence, and understanding all of which would be rather useless if permanently circumscribed by artificially imposed limits that could not be, well, penetrated by their OWN transcending capacities.

One of the upshots of this is that no one hardly dares either to refer to such transcending capacities as illogical, or to stigmatize them as irrational.

331

There are many other identified and named transcending conceptual realities that have undergone the same treatment, especially so during the latter decades of the modern era.

This has been so culturally corrosive that individuals who, in modern times, spontaneously experience a transcending phenomenon might think they have gone bonkers, have failed to identify with what is considered "normal," and might even go for recommended "cures" to get rid of such.

Even so, from ancient times onward, a plentitude of transcending conceptual realities has been recognized as such, and in different languages, have been assigned a name that denotes a specific transcending entity.

In cases where the products of such entities turned out to

be little more than imaginative flights of fancy or of delirium, of too much drink, or of unstable reality boxes, such did not automatically imply that transcending conceptual realities did not exist per se.

332

In English, some several dozens of transcending conceptual realities have been recognized and assigned dictionary terms and names that seem appropriate to their functions. A short list follows just ahead.

With respect to wisdom and wisdom-making, such must first fundamentally depend on observable, objective facts, situations, and conditions.

But these do not automatically reveal the intrinsic Ways in which they will develop, what instabilities or stabilities might result, and what ultimate outcomes might transpire. Thus, wisdom and wisdom-making must utilize some kind of transcending penetration systems.

In fact, if one examines the working nature of all transcending conceptual realities known to be identified as such, all of them represent vehicles for this or that kind of penetration system.

Transcending awareness
Transcending intelligence
Transcending innateness
Transcending compassion
Transcending empathy
Transcending discernment
Transcending insight
Transcending apprehension
Transcending interpretation
Transcending understanding
Transcending mental thought
Transcending cognition
Transcending cognizance
Transcending kenning
Transcending instinct
Transcending paralogy (the study of inherent essence and the

intrinsic)
Transcending reason
Transcending logic
Transcending contemplation
Transcending inspection
Transcending sight or view
Transcending perception
Transcending recognition
Transcending perception of motive or action
Transcending spiritual perception
Transcending vision
Transcending knowledge
Transcending philosophy
Transcending beholding
Transcending mental perception
Immediate apprehension transcending reason
Not acquired by learning
Transcending innateness
Obvious to the intuitive senses
Transcending clairvoyance
Transcending telepathy

A rather longer list of such conceptual realities has been presented earlier in pages. Such conceptual realities can easily be preceded by the term "transcending."

SIX SAYINGS ABOUT THE SIX DEGENERATIONS

- *Love of Goodness without love of learning degenerates into silliness.*
- *Love of wisdom without love of learning degenerates into utter lack of principle.*
- *Love of keeping promises without love of learning degenerates into villainy.*
- *Love of uprightness without love of learning degenerates into harshness.*
- *Love of courage without love of learning degenerates into turbulence.*
- *Love of courage without love of learning degenerates into mere recklessness.*

The venerable
CONFUCIUS
(c.551-479? B.C.)
ANALECTS, Book XVII, Section 8

Selected Bibliography

(NOTE: Following is a short list of sources that have been meaningful to the discussions in this book. Those marked with the double asterisk (**) are especially meaningful.)

Assmann, Jan, THE MIND OF EGYPT: HISTORY AND MEANING IN THE TIME OF THE PHARAOHS, (Henry Holt and Company, New York, 1996).

Bandler, Richard, and John Grinder, THE STRUCTURE OF MAGIC: A BOOK ABOUT LANGUAGE AND THERAPY, (Science and Behavior Books, Ind., Palo Alto, California, 1975).

Benton, William E., MAN-MAKING – FROM OUT OF THE MISTS TO BEYOND THE VEIL, (John M. Watkins, London, 1919).

Bergler, Edmund, THE SUPEREGO – UNCONSCIOUS CONSCIENCE, (Grune & Stratton, New York, 1952).

Bush, Vannevar, SCIENCE IS NOT ENOUGH: REFLECTIONS FOR THE PRESENT AND FUTURE, (William Morrow & Co., 1967).

Campbell, Joseph, CREATIVE MYTHOLOGY, (The Viking Press, Inc., New York, 1968).

Campbell, Joseph, Ed., MAN AND TIME: PAPERS FROM THE ERANOS YEARBOOKS, (Bollingen Series XXX,Pantheon Books, New York, 1957).

Capra, Fritjof, UNCOMMON WISDOM, (Simon and Schuster, New York,1988).

Carrel, Alexis, MAN THE UNKNOWN, (Harper & Brothers, New York, 1935).

Cirlot, J.E., A DICTIONARY OF SYMBOLS, (Philosophical Library, New York, 1974).

**Dixon, Norman, PRECONSCIOUS PROCESSING, (John Wiley 85 Sons, New York, 1981).

Editors of Pensee, VELIKOVSKY RECONSIDERED, (Doubleday, New York, 1976).

Fields, Rick, HOW THE SWANS CAME TO THE LAKE: A NARRATIVE HISTORY OF BUDDHISM IN AMERICA, (Shambhala, Boulder, Colorado, 1981).

Flenn, Jerome Clayton, FUTURE MIND: ARTIFICIAL INTELLIGENCE– MERGING THE MYSTICAL AND THE TECHNOLOGICAL IN THE 21st CENTURY, (Acropolis Books, Washington, D.C., 1989).

Garrett, Eileen J., TELEPATHY: IN SEARCH OF A LOST FACULTY, (Creative Age Press, New York, 1945).

Gaskell, G.A., DICTIONARY OF ALL SCRIPTURES AND MYTHS, (Julian Press, New York, 1950).

Gray, William G., A SELF MADE BY MAGIC, (Samuel Weiser, Inc., New York, 1976).

Grudin, Robert, THE GRACE OF GREAT THINGS: CREATIVITY AND INNOVATION, (Ticknor & Fields, New York, 1990).

Hampden-Turner, Charles, MAPS OF THE MIND: CHARTS AND CONCEPTS OF THE MIND AND ITS LABYRINTHS, (Macmillan, New York, 1981).

Heidegger, Martin, BEING AND TIME, (Harper & Row, New York, 1962).

**Hutchinson, Robert, WEAPONS OF MASS DESTRUCTION – THE NON-NONSENSEGUIDE TO NUCLEAR, CHEMICAL AND BIOLOGICAL WEAPONS TODAY, (Sterling Publishing Co., New York, 2003).

Ingalese, Richard, THE HISTORY AND POWER OF MIND, (L.N. Fowler & Co., London, 19th Edition, 1967).

**Jung, Carl G., THE ARCHETYPES OF THE COLLECTIVE UNCONSCIOUS, (Bollingen Series XX, Pantheon Books, New York, 1959.)

**Kim, Steven H., DESIGNING INTELLIGENCE: A FRAMEWORK FOR SMART SYSTEMS, (Oxford University Press, New York, 1990).

Koestler, Arthur, THE GHOST IN THE MACHINE: [A classic examination of the source of man's greatest predicament: the human mind], (Random House, New York, 1967, 1976).

Laucks, Irving F., A SPECULATION IN REALITY, (Philosophical Library, New York, 1953).

**LaViolette, Paul, EARTH UNDER FIRE: HUMANITY'S SURVIVAL OF THE APOCALYPSE, (Starburst Publications, Schenectady, New York, 1997).

Lay, Wilfrid, MAN'S UNCONSCIOUS SPIRIT, (Kegan Paul, Trench Trubner & Co., London, 1921).

Lovgren, George K., THE ART OF INNER SEEING, Karl Bem Publishers, Sun City, Arizona, 1977).

**MacIver, Robert M., POWER TRANSFORMED: THE AGE-SLOW DELIVERANCE OF THE FOLK AND NOW THE POTENTIAL DELIVERANCE OF THE NATIONS FROM THE RULE OF FORCE, (Macmillian, New York, 1964).

**McDougall, William, THE GROUP MIND (A sketch of the principles of collective psychology with some attempt to apply them to the interpretation of national life and character), (G.P. Putnam, New York, 1920).

Marcuse, Herbert, ONE-DIMENSIONAL MAN, (Beacon Press, Boston, 1968).

Mitroff, Ian I., and Warren Bennis, THE UNREALITY INDUSTRY: THE DELIBERATE MANUFACTURING OF FALSEHOOD AND WHAT IT IS DOING TO OUR LIVES, (Birch Lane Press, Carol Publishing Group, New York, 1989).

Murphy, Gardner, HUMAN POTENTIALS, (Basic Books, New York, 1958).

**Norretranders, Tor, THE USER ILLUSION: CUTTING CONSCIOUSNESS DOWN TO SIZE, (Viking, New York, 1991).

Osty, Eugene, SUPERNORMAL FACULTIES IN MAN: AN EXPERIMENTAL STUDY, (Methuen & Co., London, 1923).

Pendell, Elmer, WHY DIVILIZATIONS SELF-DESTRUCT, (Howard Allen, Cape Canaveral, Florida, 1977).

**Pinker, Steven, THE BLANK SLATE: THE MODERN DENIAL OF HUMAN NATURE, (Viking, New York, 2002).

**Rees, Martin, OUR FINAL HOUR: A SCIENTISTS WARNING: HOW TERROR, ERROR, AND ENVIRONMENTAL DISASTER THREATEN HUMANKIND'S FUTURE IN THIS CENTURY - ON EARTH AND BEYOND, (Basic Books, New York, 2003).

**Richardson, Ken, THE MAKING OF INTELLIGENCE, (Weidenfield & Nicolson, London, 1999).

Richards, E. G., MAPPING TIME: THE CALENDAR AND ITS HISTORY, (Oxford University Press, New York, 1998).

**Rivlin, Robert and Karen Gravelle, DECIPHERING THE SENSES: THE EXPANDING WORLD OF HUMAN PERCEPTION, (Simon and Schuster, New York, 1984).

Ryback, David DREAMS THAT COME TRUE - THEIR PSYCHIC AND TRANSFORMING POWERS, (Doubleday, New York, 1988).

Segal, Ronald, THE STRUGGLE AGAINST HISTORY: FROM WORLD VIOLENCE TO THE NEW CREATIVE UTOPIA, (Bantam, New York, 1973).

**Sheldrake, Rupert, THE SENSE OF BEING STARED AT: AND OTHER ASPECTS OF THE EXTENDED MIND, (Crown Publishers, New York, 2003).

Smith, Huston, BEYOND THE POST-MODERN MIND, (Theosophical Publishing House, Wheaton, Illinois, 1982).

Snider, Denton J., FEELING: PROLEGOMENA TO PSYCHOLOGY, (Sigma Publishing Co., St. Louis, 1905).

Sri Aurobindo, THE LIFE DIVINE, (Greystone Press, New York, 1949).

Strombert, Gustaf, THE SOUL OF THE UNIVERSE, (David McKay Company, 1940).

Targ, Russell & Harold Puthoff, MIND-REACH: SCIENTISTS LOOK AT PSYCHIC ABILITY, (Delacorte Press/Eleanor Friede, New York, 1977.)

Todeschi, Kevin J., THE ENCYCLOPEDIA OF SYMBOLISM, (Perigee, New York, 1995).

Trine, Ralph Waldo, IN TUNE WITH THE INFINITE – OR, FULLNESS OF PEACE, POWER, AND PLENTY, (G. Bell and Sons, London, 1960 [originally published in 1897].

Tybert, Judith M., THE LANGUAGE OF THE GODS: SANSKRIT KEYS TO INDIA'S WISDOM, (East-West Cultural Center, Los Angeles, 1970, 1976).

**Velikovsky, Immanuel, MANKIND IN AMNESIA: AN INQUIRY INTO THE FUTURE OF THE HUMAN RACE, (Doubleday & Company, Garden City, New York, 1982).

White, Stewart Edward, THE UNOBSTRUCTED UNIVERSE, (E. P. Dutton & Co., 1940.)

Yatri, UNKNOWN MAN: THE MYSTERIOUS BIRTH OF A NEW SPECIES, (Simon & Schuster, New York, 1988).

Zukav, Gary, THE DANCING WU LI MASTERS: AN OVERVIEW OF THE NEW PHYSICS, (William Morrow, New York, 1979).

A BIOMIND SUPERPOWERS BOOK FROM
SWANN-RYDER PRODUCTIONS, LLC

www.ingoswann.com

OTHER BOOKS BY INGO SWANN

Everybody's Guide to Natural ESP
Penetration
Psychic Literacy
Psychic Sexuality
Purple Fables
Reality Boxes
Secrets of Power, Volume 1
Secrets of Power, Volume 2
Star Fire
The Great Apparitions of Mary
The Psychic Child
The Windy Song
Your Nostradamus Factor

CPSIA information can be obtained
at www.ICGtesting.com
Printed in the USA
LVHW030928201119
637820LV00003B/234/P